JUST ONE VERSE

The Book of Mormon
Helaman 3:35

Denalee Call Chapman

For my Mother
Connie Wheeler Call
Thank you for teaching me to
treasure the scriptures,
one verse at a time.

Nevertheless they did fast and pray oft, and did wax stronger and stronger in their humility, and firmer and firmer in the faith of Christ, unto the filling their souls with joy and consolation, yea, even to the purifying and the sanctification of their hearts, which sanctification cometh because of their yielding their hearts unto God.

(The Book of Mormon, Helaman 3:35)

JUST ONE VERSE
FOREWORD

After a dozen or so years of really interesting but contentious history in the lives of the Nephites, wherein honest government leaders are assassinated, the city's defense goes all to pot, wars are fought, battles are lost and battles are won, Helaman II becomes the Chief Judge. Ruling in righteousness, Helaman's safety becomes threatened by Kishkumen (leader of the band of the Gandianton Robbers). But because of the loyalty of Helaman's close servant, the plot is discovered and in the end, it is Kishkumen who is killed, leaving Helaman to rule in peace. A few years of comfort followed, wherein there was no contention in the land. Helaman continued to rule in righteousness and to raise his two sons, Nephi and Lehi, to love and respect the Lord and to live His gospel. The church flourished, welcoming many converts. As is the case throughout the Book of Mormon and in all of the world's history, as people prospered, pride entered their hearts causing a division amongst them. With that division came persecution.

JUST ONE VERSE
PREFACE

My mother, who upon returning from back-to-back missions for The Church of Jesus Christ of Latter-day Saints with my father, seeking to continue mission standards and growth, chose a few dozen scriptures to memorize. A year or so earlier her son-in-law passed away. The speaker at his funeral shared great words of comfort, quoting memorized scripture and other inspirational words. This speaker was a dear friend to my mother – a person she already was working to emulate. And so, at the conclusion of my parents' missions, my mother printed select verses of scripture, artfully designed, and began memorizing. Through the years she would pull out these pages of cardstock and begin the memorization process yet again.

It was during a visit with my parents, who live several states away, that my mother and I came across this stack of printed scripture verses. We selected one at random and spent many moments throughout the week helping each other memorize. I learned through the memorization of that one verse that there is great value in focusing so intently on just one verse. I had to really think hard to repeat specific words in their rightful order. That thinking created word pictures for me and I came to understand on a much deeper level the value of those words to me, personally. I found myself pondering the reason for combining two seemingly disconnected words into one sentence. As I thought more and more about it, the scripture verse took on an entirely new meaning. It was like a light bulb had been switched on and a new world of study opened up to me. I realized that I could spend hours, even days and longer, studying, praying about, pondering, putting into practice, researching, praying some more – about this one single verse. It changed my life, really. All of a sudden I began to "treasure, not read, not study, not search, but treasure up the

Lord's word. Possess[ing] it, mak[ing] it [mine] by both believing it and knowing it . . ."[i]

Although I moved on from that one verse of scripture to study, memorize, ponder on and pray about other verses of scripture, I have the firm feeling that I'll be going back to it at some future date. I know that as I learn bit-by-bit, and move forward on my path toward Heavenly Father, when I next return to that one verse I will be ready to peel away more layers and find even deeper meaning than I found this first time around. And so it is for all of us as we make the scriptures a part of our daily lives. As President Gordon B. Hinckley promised, "your minds will be enlightened and your spirits will be lifted."[ii] Elder Richard G. Scott encouraged us: "Scriptures are like packets of light that illuminate our minds and give place to guidance and inspiration from on high."[iii]

I think of verses of scripture as power-packed vitamins. We daily feast on the scriptures as a whole . . . but when we take just one verse and truly treasure it, our spirits are nourished in a way that will sustain us, help us grow, and keep us firmly on our paths of progression.

This book is a peek into the impact that a few verses of scripture have had on me. It is my hope that through reading *Just One Verse* the infectious joy of treasuring up the Lord's word will permeate your soul, and you will be prompted, as I have, to examine individual verses of scripture and discover the personal meaning the Lord intends for you to find.

[i] Bruce R. McConkie, Doctrinal New Testament Commentary, Vol. 1 pg. 662
[ii] Gordon B. Hinckley, April 1995 LDS General Conference, "The Light Within You"
[iii] Richard G. Scott, October 2001 LDS General Conference, "The Power of Scripture"

NEVERTHELESS

I ask myself: *When times are hard or when I'm treated unfairly, do I have a "nevertheless principle" as an automatic action to take?* So often it's easy, and even comfortable, to ride the current and let the flow take me where it will. One of Satan's big lies is that our natural reaction is something we can't control. When someone accuses me, my natural reaction may be to become defensive and accuse right back; when everything appears to be falling apart, my natural reaction may be to become bitter, self-absorbed, and even whiny. But with a "nevertheless principle" firmly planted in my heart and in my mind, my natural inclination will change. Instead of automatically *reacting* negatively, I will instead be proactive. I will act in strength with the power of the Lord supporting me to fight against the hardship which is attacking me.

Certainly the greatest example of living "nevertheless" perfectly is Christ in the Garden of Gethsemane. His suffering, although just beginning, was intense. "And he went a little further, and fell on his face, and prayed, saying, O my Father, if it be possible, let this cup pass from me: *nevertheless* not as I will, but as thou wilt."[1] This one verse of scripture teaches us that when we are understanding the purpose of our lives, and when we are humbly filled with desire to live the unique mission Heavenly Father has planned for us individually, "nevertheless" is an action that will lead us further along the right path. That will happen, not only *in spite of* hardship that comes our way, but most assuredly *because* of that adversity.

Young Nephi taught us how important it is to make "nevertheless" a natural reaction. He and his brothers were required to enter a hostile situation in order to secure the Brass Plates.[2] They had already experienced some unsuccessful attempts with requesting, then even offered to purchase the sacred historical records. In spite of this, they were unable to get them. Yet Nephi would not be thwarted. Although his very life was in danger, he would not stop until he had completed the Lord's errand. Nephi left his reluctant brothers, who were hidden outside of the city walls. Then he went solo toward Laban's house, determined to secure the plates. But he didn't have a plan this time. "And I was led by the Spirit, not knowing beforehand the things which I should do. *Nevertheless* I went forth ..."[3] Nephi acted, thus fulfilling part of his mission – an essential part that would serve to help keep his posterity grounded in the Gospel.

The scriptures are filled with examples of using the "nevertheless principle" to press forward and focus on living as Heavenly Father desires. Mortality is difficult, just because it's mortality. Even if there were no unkind people like those who began to persecute the righteous people in Helaman's time[4], mortality in and of itself would create hardship for us. Our bodies are prone to disease; there are natural calamities including floods, earthquakes, typhoons, fire and more. Being mortal means adversity and hardship will come our way. Interestingly, it's those hardships that strengthen us and help us to become refined, educated and wise. But that desired outcome will only happen as we learn to develop a "nevertheless attitude."

If I'm wise, I will have an entire arsenal of "nevertheless" weapons to draw from. But what are they, where do they come from, and how do I keep ready access to them? As always, the scriptures have the answers. In one of his epistles to the Ephesians, Paul the apostle taught, "Put on the whole armour of God, that ye may be able to stand against the wiles of the devil."[5] And then, emphasizing the importance of this, he goes on to say, "Wherefore take unto you the whole armour of God, that ye may be able to withstand in the evil day, and having done all, to stand. Stand therefore, having your loins girt about with truth, and having on the breastplate of righteousness; And your feet shod with the preparation of the gospel of peace; Above all, taking the shield of faith, wherewith ye shall be able to quench all the fiery darts of the wicked. And take the helmet of salvation, and the sword of the Spirit, which is the word of God."[6] The necessity of taking armor and weapons to ensure our progression and exaltation was reiterated by the Lord through the Prophet Joseph Smith: "Wherefore, lift up your hearts and rejoice, and gird up your loins, and take upon you my whole armor, that ye may be able to withstand the evil day, having done all, that ye may be able to stand."[7] It is meaningful that included in this revelation to the Prophet, we are first counseled to "lift up your hearts and rejoice." Part of pressing forward in mortality is experiencing joy. Yes! Joy even in the midst of hardship is doable. Joy, even as we are preparing ourselves for battle, or in the middle of a battle, is attainable. In part, it is joy that helps us to "endure it well."[8]

Our "nevertheless" weapons should include truth, faith, testimony, scripture study and prayer. But we are individuals with individual weakness and individual hardship. Because of that, we may have specific weapons – in addition to the armor that is required for all. "Nevertheless weapons" specific to individuals may include things like:

- ☐ Think before I speak
- ☐ Purge myself of anger
- ☐ Count my blessings
- ☐ Do an act of service every day
- ☐ Eliminate swearing
- ☐ Notice something positive about my family members and tell them regularly
- ☐ Obey the speed limit
- ☐ Be on time for everything

- ☐ Get proper sleep
- ☐ Record my personal thoughts in a weekly journal

The list could go on for pages because there are as many weaknesses just waiting to become strengths as there are people in this world! It can get overwhelming if we are prone to guilt ourselves into change. The Lord doesn't want that. But He does want us to progress, to recognize our weaknesses, to be humble and ask for help, and then to act on the changes we feel *inspired* to make. Inspiration is an entirely different force than guilt. Inspiration to change will give us a feeling of peace and excitement. We will look forward to the work required to turn our recently revealed weakness into a strength when that inspiration comes from the Lord. "Tomorrow's joy or tomorrow's despair has its roots in decisions we make today. Perhaps some people think to themselves, 'I know I need to change some things in my life. Maybe later, but not now.' Those who stand at the threshold of life always waiting for the right time to change are like the man who stands at the bank of a river waiting for the water to pass so he can cross on dry land. *Today is the day of decision.*"[9]

Just as weapons are forged, so our "nevertheless" actions need to be developed. We have the tools and the instructions, but we must do the work. When we do our part, our efforts are magnified by the grace of God and our arsenal of weapons becomes strong. In addition, it becomes natural for us to draw on those weapons rather than to retreat. We are taught, "Help from the Savior is available for the entire journey of mortality—from bad to good to better and to change our very nature."[10] I love knowing that our natures can be changed! As we pray to understand our weaknesses, particularly those that we should tackle right now, we will be led to not only recognize what needs to be changed, but also *how* to change. Additionally, when we are humbly seeking instruction from the Lord, inspiration and revelation will be granted to us even when we aren't expecting it. Elder Richard G. Scott taught us the difference between inspiration and revelation: "The Holy Ghost communicates important information that we need to guide us in our mortal journey. When it is crisp and clear and essential, it warrants the title of revelation. When it is a series of promptings we often have to guide us step by step to a worthy objective, for the purpose of this message, it is inspiration."[11] Later, in this conference address, Elder Scott said, "We receive help from our Father in Heaven in response to our faith, obedience, and the proper use of agency." I've had experiences wherein I've received inspiration regarding my own weaknesses as I've had that thought forefront in my mind. It amazes me each time I feel a direct answer – words in my mind – come to me during something completely unrelated to study, prayer or pondering. But this happens because of the work I have already done. Often, I will have been praying for guidance for days, weeks, or longer. Then, when the inspiration comes, it is very clear. I have been working on getting the answer for long enough that it never really leaves my mind.

Consider the young piano student who practices a single measure, over and over and over again. She also goes to school, eats meals and plays with friends. But every day she spends time at the piano trying to perfect that one measure of music. Finally, after a full week of practice, she sits down at her friend's piano just for fun. Imagine her delight when the very measure she couldn't quite master through her practice all of a sudden is played perfectly, almost without thought. She put in the time, she put in the work, and quite likely she had moments of discouragement. Then finally it paid off. This is how inspiration may work for us sometimes. As we ponder and consider what we should practice, in order that we might add to our arsenal of "nevertheless" weapons, we will be guided. It is also important to note that once inspiration is given, it is expected that we will act on that inspiration. President Boyd K.

Packer taught, "Each of us must stay in condition to respond to inspiration and the promptings of the Holy Ghost. The Lord has a way of pouring pure intelligence into our minds to prompt us, to guide us, to teach us, and to warn us. Each son or daughter of God can know the things they need to know instantly. Learn to receive and act on inspiration and revelation."[12] And Elder Richard G. Scott clarified the method to continue to receive inspiration when he told us: "When we receive an impression in our heart, we can use our mind either to rationalize it away or to accomplish it. Be careful what you do with an impression from the Lord."[13] At another LDS General Conference, Elder Boyd K. Packer taught us that we must act upon the inspiration we receive: "This voice of the Spirit speaks gently, prompting you what to do or what to say, or it may caution or warn you. Ignore or disobey these promptings, and the Spirit will leave you. It is your choice—your agency."[14]

I know an individual who has the remarkable gift of recognition and ability to change. But she wasn't always this way. I asked her about this gift a few years ago. She told me that she realizes that it is through the Atonement that she recognized that there are a lot of things more important than appearances. She came to desire, from deep within her heart, to be pure before the Lord. She stopped taking offense when criticized, and instead carefully considered what was said to her. Then she would take what the Spirit confirmed to be truth, throw out the rest, and move forward resolutely to make the suggested changes. Whether the criticizer meant to help her or hurt her didn't matter and doesn't matter. She is simply concerned with what *she* needs to do and think and feel. I've watched this remarkable young woman as weak things have not just become strong, they've become positive characteristics that stand out so boldly that people describing her character would definitely mention them. When I've had opportunity to spend a few days at a time with her, I have been in awe as I've watched the process. She is, more than anyone I know, in a constant state of change. It seems that daily she is alerted to something she desires to do better – and then she sets her mind to it and intentionally works on it ... *beginning immediately.* This is what conversion is. This is the way I am striving to be. It is this type of preparation that will give us enough "nevertheless" weapons that we will be able to be proactive and move forward rather than riding the current backward.

When we make a habit of daily morning and evening prayers we will be more likely to ask for help that day to be strong as we attack the weakness we are currently working toward changing. When we do that the Lord is with us. We will recognize opportunities to practice making our desired changes. My experience is that the change usually doesn't happen all at once. In fact, for me it gets harder before it gets easier. But I testify that when I focus on one or two weaknesses that are especially obvious to me, mortality throws many opportunities my way to change them. Perhaps it's simply because I'm aware – or perhaps Satan tries to weaken me with repeated difficulties – or perhaps the Lord is blessing me with plenty of chances to practice. Whatever the reason, when I am self-aware and accepting of the assistance the Lord is already willing to give, I am then able to build up weapons to place in my arsenal. With a quiver of "nevertheless weapons" at the ready, I am prepared to be proactive with the Lord by my side as I conquer the adversity that comes my way.

As we consider the state of those in Helaman's day who, through no fault of their own, were persecuted and bombarded with adversity, we may find that life for us is much the same. Whether our attackers are obvious or stealthy, Satan has each of us in his sights. He wants to stop our forward progression – he wants to damn us. Satan wants us to be miserable like he is. But we are blessed with the agency and the power to fight him. Embracing a "nevertheless principle" by donning appropriate armor will empower us to be proactive. Our natures will be changed so we can "lift up [our] hearts and rejoice" as we "withstand the evil day."

[1] New Testament, Matthew 26:39 (italics added)

[2] The Book of Mormon, 1 Nephi 3 & 4

[3] The Book of Mormon, 1 Nephi 4:6-7 (italics added)

[4] The Book of Mormon, Helaman 3:35

[5] New Testament, Ephesians 6:11

[6] New Testament, Ephesians 6:13-17

[7] Doctrine and Covenants 27:15-18

[8] Doctrine and Covenants 121:8

[9] LDS General Conference, October 2003, Three Choices, Joseph B. Wirthlin (italics added)

[10] LDS General Conference, April 2012, The Atonement and the Journey of Mortality, David A. Bednar

[11] LDS General Conference, April 2012, How to Obtain Revelation and Inspiration for Your Personal Life, Richard G. Scott

[12] LDS General Conference, April 2013, These Things I Know, Boyd K. Packer

[13] LDS General Conference, October 1989, Learning to Recognize Answers to Prayers, Richard G. Scott

[14] LDS General Conference, October 1994, Personal Revelation: The Gift, The Test, The Promise, Boyd K. Packer

THEY DID FAST AND PRAY OFT

The scriptures are filled with examples of individuals who fasted and prayed. Our modern world is as well. In the New Testament, Matthew 17:21, Jesus taught that some things are so monumental that we need the power of fasting combined with prayer to get results.[1] But in the context of the scripture we're studying, there was not a single episode that needed "fixing." Rather, the people who were being persecuted did not give in to peer pressure, did not revile against those who were persecuting them, but they "did fast and pray oft." It was a regular practice of theirs. We know that making a daily habit of prayer is beneficial to us. Not that Heavenly Father needs to hear from us, but that *we* need to pray. "As soon as we learn the true relationship in which we stand toward God (namely, God is our Father, and we are his children), then at once prayer becomes natural and instinctive on our part. Many of the so-called difficulties about prayer arise from forgetting this relationship. Prayer is the act by which the will of the Father and the will of the child are brought into correspondence with each other. The object of prayer is not to change the will of God, but to secure for ourselves and for others blessings that God is already willing to grant, but that are made conditional on our asking for them. Blessings require some work or effort on our part before we can obtain them. Prayer is a form of work, and is an appointed means for obtaining the highest of all blessings."[2] It is true that for those who are in tune to the true relationship we have with Heavenly Father, constant prayer is instinctual. When happy moments arise, we may offer an instant silent prayer of thanks. When confused or concerned, we may immediately turn to Heavenly Father in prayer for direction. When we remember our relationship with Heavenly Father, we won't feel alone – we'll be inclined to reach out in prayer at all times throughout the day. I think of Amulek becoming a missionary companion to Alma and understanding so clearly his relationship to Heavenly Father and Jesus Christ that he risked everything to share that knowledge. Amulek taught that we should pray over everything, and pray all the time![3] And he told us how to do that: "Yea, and when you do not cry unto the Lord, let your hearts be full, drawn out in prayer unto him continually ..."[4] We live in a mortal world where we must spend time doing mortal things. We work, we study, we clean, we talk, we exercise, we eat, and more. But that doesn't mean our hearts can't be involved in prayer. They can. It's something that can be practiced to the point of our very natures becoming prayerful. We can become praying people who turn to the Lord immediately in thanksgiving or in pleading. It is part of the Atonement – for our natures to be drawn to God.

Jesus Christ, Himself, taught us how to pray. Matthew recorded the Lord's instructions as He taught His disciples how to pray.[5] The Christian world knows this teaching as *The Lord's Prayer*. I love the verse that precedes the actual prayer. " ... your Father knoweth what things ye have need of before ye ask him."[6] And yet, Jesus then goes on to ask for needful things ("Give us this day our daily bread ... forgive us ..."[7]). Even though our Father already knows what we need. Interesting. This is so obviously instructional! Heavenly Father knows what we need. It is important that we ask for what we need. And it's important that we pray in specifics. Remember Amulek's instructions about prayer: "Cry unto him for mercy ... over all your flocks ... over all your household ... against the power of your enemies ..."[8] How do we do this without trying to bend God's will to our desires? How do we pray with specific requests without sounding like we know best? That's been a challenge for me. Experience has taught me that what matters is where our hearts are. In other words, do I have my heart set on the things of this world, and I want what I want no matter what? Or do I focus my hope on eternity and truly, deep down, want what Heavenly Father knows is best for me? If I can answer honestly in the affirmative to the last question, I am then able to pray in specifics with the peace of mind that Heavenly Father will grant the request if it is part of His plan, but if not, I will be blessed in the way He desires. There are times when I've felt such a clear impression to pray for something boldly specific. The feeling has been strong and clear. When I've followed the prompting, I've seen miraculous fulfillment of the request. I have been grateful that I've had the courage at those times to ask in specifics. I'll illustrate with another person's experience recently shared with me and used with his permission:

I've been blessed to spend time as an adult with my parents. Included in my many visits have been weekly trips to the temple during their Wednesday night shift. As temple workers, my parents have made lasting friendships with some incredible people. Dallas Temple Sealer, Tim O'Brien and his wife, Debby, were preparing to leave on a mission. While I was visiting my parents, the couple was invited over for a visit before their departure. During dinner as the couples updated each other about their families, Tim gave us some background on their oldest son. At age 18 their son hit a rebellious streak and left the Church. He moved out and Tim and Debby would go weeks without hearing from him. When he did make an appearance he was often accompanied by some shady friends who confirmed the O'Briens' concern that their son was making some very poor choices. These good parents continued to love and pray for their son and to be grateful for any contact they had. Debby prayed specifically that he would be kept safe during this time, however long it would be. She greatly desired that his mortal life be prolonged, giving him time to learn what he must. One night at the temple Tim felt an urgency to pray for their son. He entered the Celestial room and bowed his head in silent prayer. As he began his prayer for his son the thought came: *Pray to hear from him tonight.* Humbly, Tim did just that. He prayed that after these few months of no contact, their son would call *that night.* After the shift ended he asked Debby, "Has he called you today?" He hadn't. Then Tim told Debby what he'd done. It wasn't long before the call came. Tim answered the phone and asked his son, "Why did you call? Why now?" "I don't know," he said, "a couple of hours ago I just knew I needed to call." Of course, the prompting came to their son at the very time Tim was praying for him. Tim bore testimony to his son that Heavenly Father heard and answered his prayer, that Heavenly Father knows him and loves him. Parents and son spent a tender few minutes on the phone. Time went by, and their son continued in his destructive habits. Again, weeks passed with no contact. Once again at the temple, Tim felt the same promptings, took the same actions, and was blessed with the same results. Their son is now active in his testimony and has a beautiful family. Tim and Debby were bold as they prayed in specifics according to the promptings they received and their desires.

When our oldest son was serving his mission in Russia, I would often wake up in the night with a prompting to pray. I would roll over onto my knees and offer a prayer with very specific requests for protection and direction for my son. It wasn't until years after his mission that I learned of some of the scary situations he experienced. I know that at those moments I was given the desire to pray and what to pray for. Although I will never know exactly how each prayer was answered, I do know that my son came home, testimony intact and physically safe.

I've also had experiences when I've prayed with very specific requests that have not been granted. But I truly meant it when I added to my prayer the "but if not" phrase. Remember Shadrach, Meshach and Abed-nego who were thrown into the fiery furnace by orders of King Nebuchadnezzar? They refused to bow down and worship the king's golden image. But the men were firm in their faith. When the king threatened them with death by fire they responded, "If it be so, our God whom we serve is able to deliver us from the burning fiery furnace, and he will deliver us out of thine hand, O king. *But if not*, be it known unto thee, O king, that we will not serve thy gods, nor worship the golden image which thou has set up."[9] I love the courage of these men. Though the prayers of these three men are not recorded, I'm sure they asked in specifics for protection. I'm equally sure they were completely willing to accept whatever Heavenly Father willed.

I haven't experienced anything nearly so dramatic as Shadrach, Meshach and Abed-nego. But I have felt honest acceptance of Heavenly Father's will while praying in specifics. For years we were a one-car family. In my mind, life is easier that way. Fewer repairs, less money in gas and insurance, and more room in the garage. Well, our one car - which we had pampered in every way for years - was in an accident. I loved that car. After it was towed to the body shop I knelt in prayer and asked very specifically that the car be repairable and be returned to us for more great years of usage. I added, "*but if not*, please direct us to find the means to be able to get where we need to go each day." I meant it. When the call came in from the insurance company's Total Loss Department my heart sunk. I took a deep breath and prepared to move forward as we searched for a car. In the end, this was a great blessing for us as we were able to purchase two amazing vehicles with the settlement money. I never would have thought to ask for the car to be a total loss and for us to be able to buy two to replace it! But I have learned to really want what Heavenly Father knows is best for me.

The people of Helaman's time fasted and prayed "oft." Just how often does "oft" mean? If we are always in the attitude of prayer, and in the habit of regular fasting, how likely will we be to be able to function well when hardship hits? Well, I suppose none of us can know how often the people of Helaman's time fasted. But aren't we blessed to have monthly fasts scheduled in the restored Church? Doesn't it seem that if we make prayer and fasting a habit when life is going well that we will be stronger and more able to handle adversity when it comes along, as it surely will? Think of the person who exercises on a regular basis. She walks daily, lifts weights regularly, and makes sure to get her stretches in. How much more ready and able will she be to lift the fallen entertainment center off her child? That's the way it is for us with prayer and fasting. When a crisis hits, if we have made honest prayer a part of our nature and have incorporated fasting into our lives, we will naturally be drawn to Heavenly Father in the way that will be most beneficial for our growth, our guidance and our much desired peace.

I'm reminded of the people who were baptized by Alma at the Waters of Mormon. They felt the Spirit as they were taught eternal truths.[10] These were praying people[11] who were taken into bondage, not because of wickedness, but just because wicked people sought to rule over them. "And it came to pass that so great were their afflictions that they began to cry mightily to God."[12] These good people had made praying such a part of their lives that when Amulon commanded them to stop praying and threatened to kill any who were caught praying, they "did pour out their hearts to him; and he did know the thoughts of their hearts."[13] Their prayers for deliverance weren't immediately answered with deliverance, but Heavenly Father answered them in the way He knew was best for them. "And now it came to pass that the burdens which were laid upon Alma and his brethren were made light; yea, the Lord did strengthen them that they could bear up their burdens with ease, and they did submit cheerfully and with patience to all the will of the Lord."[14] The people were eventually delivered from bondage and set free. But not until they had experienced some real hardship and some incredible miracles, and great growth.

Becoming a person who does "fast and pray oft" is a matter of will power. We make up our minds to do it, then we act. We refuse to move on with our day until we've knelt in prayer; we stop ourselves from beginning our meal until gratitude has been expressed and a blessing asked; we step outside of the contentious room and offer a silent plea for the Spirit; we drop to our knees in gratitude when a sweet miracle is revealed; and more. As we do so over and over again, it becomes a part of who we are. At that point, we no longer have to think about it - it's not an intentional action anymore but rather, has become instinctual. Our natures have changed. We find ourselves praying in the car, during a difficult conversation, right before an important event, as we hear of someone's hardship and more. Sometimes we may find ourselves speaking our prayer out loud as we're alone in nature, or we find that our thoughts are in the form of prayer when others are present. When we truly desire to become a praying person, we will practice it enough to where it becomes a part of us. Developing the habit of fasting is the same. It may begin as we fast monthly because of a desire to be obedient. When a family difficulty arises we might be prompted to offer to fast with/for the individual experiencing the problem. When an answer to prayer is slow in coming, we may turn to fasting as a way to enhance our prayers. Fasting then becomes part of our natures.

I love the Lord's comparison offered in the Doctrine and Covenants section 59 as He teaches us about the Sabbath Day. He compares fasting with joy. In fact, in verse fourteen He tells us that "fasting" is synonymous with "rejoicing."[15] That is one of those mysteries that can't be understood until experienced. How is going without food joyful? Isaiah recorded the Lord's patient reaction to those who complained about fasting. They wanted to know why God didn't see them suffering with hunger pangs and reward them accordingly. Certainly it was clear to everyone around them that they were fasting - why couldn't God see it? His answer in Isaiah is echoed throughout the scriptures, "Is not this the fast that I have chosen? to loose the bands of wickedness, to undo the heavy burdens, and to let the oppressed go free, and that ye break every yoke? Is it not to deal thy bread to the hungry, and that thou bring the poor that are cast out to thy house? when thou seest the naked, that thou cover him; and that thou hide not thyself from thine own flesh? Then shall thy light break forth as the morning, and thine health shall spring forth speedily; and thy righteousness shall go before thee; the glory of the Lord shall be thy rereward. Then shalt thou call, and the Lord shall answer; thou shalt cry, and he shall say, Here I am. If thou take away from the midst of thee the yoke, the putting forth of the finger, and speaking vanity; And if thou draw out thy soul to the hungry, and satisfy the afflicted soul; then shall thy light rise in obscurity, and thy darkness be as the noonday: And the Lord shall guide thee continually, and satisfy thy soul in drought, and make fat thy bones: and thou shalt be like a watered garden, and like a spring of water, whose waters fail not."[16] Fasting, to be efficacious, must be accompanied by a heart and actions that are reaching out to others. As mentioned earlier, the Book of Mormon prophet, Amulek, taught that we must pray over everything. But then he offers this caution: "And now behold, my beloved brethren, I say unto you, do not suppose that this is all; for after ye have done all these things, if ye turn away the needy, and the naked, and visit not the sick and afflicted, and impart of your substance, if ye have, to those who stand in need - I say unto you, if ye do not any of these things, behold, your prayer is vain, and availeth you nothing, and ye are as hypocrites who do deny the faith."[17] These scriptures are supported by others[18] and teach us that if we would have fasting be a joyful experience, it must be accompanied by service of some sort. This can include generous fast offerings, reaching out to someone in need, heartfelt and sincere prayers for another, and more. The hunger pangs may still be present when we go without food - but the experience will feel happy.

Have you ever been surprised when doing something mundane for a person in need? It's so different than when you're doing it for yourself. For example, are you one of those who actually enjoys the fresh air and great feeling of shoveling snow from your neighbor's sidewalk, but just can't find the fun in doing your own? All of life is like that, really. When we're doing for someone else with an honest desire to serve, joy is an immediate reward. So it is with fasting. When our fasting is accompanied with focus on others, it becomes joyful. As we practice this, it becomes part of our nature. We will have learned to "fast and pray oft," or in other words, rejoice and pray.

The addition of fasting to prayer is like adding salt to your food. The enhancement creates obvious results. Like food - prayer - in and of itself, is nourishing and pleasant. Just as food comes alive with the addition of salt (think of eating a potato chip that hasn't been salted ... you still get the crunch, still get filled ... but when salted, the enjoyment is increased almost immeasurably!) the effect of fasting on top of praying is monumental.

When I was young one of my good friends was going through a rough time. I didn't know exactly what was happening in her life, but every now and then when I'd look at her there would be a sadness in her eyes that broke my heart. I was still struggling with desire when it came to fasting, but prayer was a strong part of my life. I prayed for my friend every day. We got together often and had a lot of fun, but there continued to be hidden pain that tainted our time together. One night when I was praying before bed, the thought came to me that I should fast for my friend. Other than family fasts, I had never fasted with personal purpose. But I loved my friend so much that I determined to do it. I began my fast immediately. The next day was Sunday (not Fast Sunday) so as far as I knew, I was the only one fasting. As we sang the opening song in Sacrament Meeting I was so filled with the Spirit. "Prayer is the soul's sincere desire, uttered or unexpressed ... Prayer is the burden of a sigh, the falling of a tear ... Prayer is the simplest form of speech ... Prayer, the sublimest strains that reach the Majesty on high .."[19] My fasting and praying may have helped my friend - I don't actually know. But what a difference it made in my life! If not for fasting that day I don't believe I would have been so open to feeling Heavenly confirmation that every prayer is heard. I wouldn't have had my testimony strengthened about my personal relationship with a Father who is aware of me and loves me. I wouldn't have been so focused on helping another that I could feel the Savior beside me. During that hymn I looked toward my friend who was not looking at me, but just straight ahead. I was close enough to see watery eyes. I knew that Heavenly Father was aware of her as much as He was aware of me at that moment. The effect of my fasting with real intent, combined with sincere prayer, was monumental for me.

I was blessed to listen in on a conversation my cousin was having with my mother. Chapter 58 in Isaiah had come up and they were discussing the blessings of fasting. Heidi said that she's really studying what Isaiah teaches about fasting because after decades of fasting regularly, she still feels like she hasn't touched the surface of that eternal principle. I was intrigued because I feel the same. With Heidi's permission, the following is the beginning of her search into the gift and power of fasting:

> Heidi grew up in a loving, structured family. With many children in the home, her parents carefully guided each day. Every member would participate in family activities, play together, pray together, attend church together and fast

monthly. Fasting was as much a part of Heidi's life as brushing her teeth. Similar to my experiences as a young girl, Heidi knew that being obedient to the Law of the Fast was the right thing to do. She made fasting a habit. Now, as a busy mother herself, Heidi has been drawn to study and learn, incorporate and internalize the deeper meaning and blessing associated with fasting. Just a few months ago she and her husband became more intentional about fasting with purpose. Instead of "getting through" the accepted two-meal-skip then ending their fast with prayer and quickly satisfying their hunger, Heidi and her husband chose to fast for three meals. They determined that every time they felt a hunger pang, it would draw their hearts to prayer, remembering the purpose of their fast. Fasting became joyful that night and day. Their hearts were focused on communion with Heavenly Father. They were humble. They recognized more strongly their reliance on the Savior, on Heavenly Guidance, and on the fact that all they have comes from God. For Heidi and Scott, fasting and prayer became "rejoicing and prayer." And, although it doesn't happen immediately for everyone all the time, the purpose of that fast was realized. For a long period of time Scott and Heidi had been paying a mortgage on the home they live in as well as the home they moved from. They did so without complaint, but with understandable financial stress. Scott and Heidi had the "but if not" attitude. But that very week - the week of their fast - they got renters in the home.

Many of us have had similar experiences as we've put the Lord to the test. While my parents were serving one of their missions in Canada, they would often end their letters with verse 10 in the Section 82 of the Doctrine and Covenants: "I the Lord am bound when ye do what I say, but when ye do not what I say ye have no promise."[20] Obedience to the Law of the Fast will bring blessings. Fasting with real intent and a desire to *understand* better and to *be* better will bring obvious blessings and internal growth.

When I read about the people of Helaman being persecuted, but fasting and praying often, I imagine they not only followed those eternal principles individually, but also as groups. When I've been involved in group fasts accompanied by prayer I've felt incredible power that is indescribable. I've seen miracles happen and when I've been the recipient of multiple people fasting and praying I've felt a peace that could calm any turmoil.

We know there is power in numbers when praying and fasting. The exemplary young Esther of the Old Testament taught us that truth. When confronted with the terrifying prospect of presenting herself before the king to "make supplication unto him, and to make request before him for her people"[21] who were threatened with destruction, Esther called upon her people to fast with her. "Go, gather together all the Jews ... and fast ye for me, and neither eat nor drink three days, night or day: I also and my maidens will fast likewise; and so will I go in unto the king, which is not according to the law: and if I perish, I perish."[22] They *did* fast and Esther *did* present herself before the king. She did so with calmness and courage. I believe the peace she carried with her was a result of the fasting and prayers. Esther was not put to death, but rather, the king welcomed her as she shared the plight of her people and uncovered the wicked plot of his advisor, Haman. Millions of lives were saved - a miracle indeed!

Surely, learning to fast and pray oft is a goal worthy of our efforts.

[1] The New Testament, Matthew 17:21 "Howbeit this kind goeth not out but by prayer and fasting."

[2] L.D.S. Bible Dictionary, Prayer

[3] The Book of Mormon, Alma 34:17-27

[4] The Book of Mormon, Alma 34:27

[5] The New Testament, Matthew 6:2-13

[6] The New Testament, Matthew 6:8

[7] The New Testament, Matthew 6:11,12

[8] The Book of Mormon, Alma 34:18,20-22

[9] The Old Testament, Daniel 3:17-18 (italics added)

[10] The Book of Mormon, Mosiah 18

[11] The Book of Mormon, Mosiah 18:23

[12] The Book of Mormon, Mosiah 24:10

[13] The Book of Mormon, Mosiah 24:12

[14] The Book of Mormon, Mosiah 24:15

[15] Doctrine and Covenants 59:12-14

[16] The Old Testament, Isaiah 58:6-11

[17] The Book of Mormon, Alma 34:28

[18] Doctrine and Covenants 104

[19] LDS Hymns #145

[20] Doctrine and Covenants 82:10

[21] The Old Testament, Esther 4:8

[22] The Old Testament, Esther 4:16

AND DID WAX STRONGER AND STRONGER IN THEIR HUMILITY

When I was working to memorize this scripture I kept getting stuck on this phrase. "Stronger" and "humility" didn't seem to go together. I had always considered humility a passive characteristic. This gave me opportunity to really consider what the phrase means. As I was memorizing I kept wanting to change the phrase to "they did become more and more humble." So it got me thinking: *Stronger and stronger in their humility.* I started to see humility in an entirely different way. I'm learning that humility is *active* rather than passive. Humility doesn't just happen to us; we work to possess it. Humility is not only intentionally cultivated, it is also an action that reaches beyond our hearts into everything we are associated with. Just as muscles become stronger and stronger as we exercise them, our humility becomes stronger and stronger as we exercise it. And we wouldn't be able to exercise it if we didn't have opportunity – that is, if we didn't have adversity or hardship. Humility is something that we *grow*, not something that we have that stays stagnant.

The dictionary lists one antonym of pride: humility.[1] President Ezra Taft Benson taught us in his General Conference talk *Beware of Pride*[2] that the antidote for pride is humility. So to understand more about humility, it helps to know what humility *isn't*. President Benson is very clear, very specific about what pride (the opposite of humility) is. "The central feature of pride is enmity – enmity toward God and enmity toward our fellowmen. Enmity means 'hatred toward, hostility to, or a state of opposition' ... Pride is essentially competitive in nature. We pit our will against God's ... Our will in competition to God's will allows desires, appetites, and passions to go unbridled ... The proud cannot accept the authority of God giving direction to their lives ... Another major portion of this very prevalent sin of pride is enmity toward our fellowmen. We are tempted daily to elevate ourselves above others and diminish them." President Benson goes on to tell us that some characteristics of pride include selfishness, contention, unrighteous dominion, abuse, disobedience, gossiping, living beyond our means, envying, withholding gratitude, being unforgiving, conceit, arrogance, and boastfulness. Wow!

So where do we start? It can seem overwhelming, sometimes, as we work to become better people. President Dieter F. Uchtdorf gave us a starting point in the 2010 General Conference: "Humility directs our attention and love toward others and to Heavenly Father's purposes. Pride does the opposite. Pride draws its energy and strength from the deep wells of selfishness. The moment we stop obsessing with ourselves and lose ourselves in service, our pride diminishes and begins to die."[3] To become humble, we have to forget ourselves and focus on others.

My daughters and I had known Tiffany for just four months when the cancer took over in her body. But it felt like we had known her a lifetime. At just 21 years old, Tiffany had been homebound for a while. Her parents had moved out of state while she was in college and became ill. So when she came home to live with her parents while receiving cancer treatments, Tiffany was lonely. She didn't have the strength to attend young adult functions, but there were a handful of individuals who visited Tiffany in her home and became her friend. The three of us were among those blessed to know her. Getting to know Tiffany was like diving into a pool of chocolate. We were saturated in fun and delicious sweetness. There was no awkward getting-to-know-you time period ... we were immediate kindred spirits. Tiffany had two other friends in the area and when they were home from college they enjoyed Tiffany's spunk as much as we did. One of those friends, Ashley, has been a best friend to my daughters for years. Ashley was home for the semester, and she and her mom, Jen, spent as much time with Tiffany and her parents as we did. It was especially fun when we were all together.

I had just returned home from traveling and stopped in to see Tiffany. She had spent a day in the hospice center earlier in the week – the pain was getting to be too much to manage at home. She was able to share only a couple of forced smiles as we visited. My daughter and I could tell the visit was wearing her out, so we kept it short. The next day she was admitted to the center again. With her parents' permission, we picked up Jen and Ashley and headed out for another visit with Tiffany – this one with her in a hospital bed. I watched as the girls gave Tiffany a manicure. Their thoughts were far from the typical concerns of young adults – no worrying about tests or how their hair looks, no concerns about dating or being left out of groups. These girls were focused on Tiffany. They were cultivating their humility. But my daughter and I were the recipients of tender service and an even greater show of humility when we drove home from the hospice center. We had just pulled into Jen and Ashley's driveway to drop them off when my phone buzzed. It was Tiffany's mother. She was dying quickly – a couple of days, or maybe just hours left. Before I could even share the news I began to weep. Really weep. My head on the steering wheel; as I cried, the others did too. Through my mind ran the scripture, "Thou shalt live together in love insomuch that thou shalt weep for the loss of them that die."[4] Yes, we loved Tiffany. Jen and Ashley loved Tiffany, but they also loved us. It was late at night, but those two good friends were in their home only minutes before they arrived back at our house. Ashley filled her bag with every imaginable candy to help her grief-stricken friend; and Jen sat on our couch with me until we had both cried ourselves dry. These two were hurting, but they knew we were hurting and came to our aid. They forgot themselves and focused on others. I can't help but think that their humility grew exponentially that night.

As we forget ourselves and focus on others we are exercising our humility and it is becoming an active, essential characteristic. Humility doesn't equal weakness ... it equals strength. When we are humble we are no longer subject to what the world thinks, what our neighbor thinks, or even what our friends think. We are subject only to God, who is our loving Heavenly Father and wants what is ultimately best for us! Humility means letting go of competition and seeking only to gratify our perfect Father - our Father who loves us, who actually wants us to succeed, and who has no ill intent. Becoming humble means becoming free. Satan loses his hold on us and our minds and hearts become focused on the things of eternity. In an interesting way, becoming humble (since this means truly desiring Heavenly Father's will over our own) takes a lot of pressure off of us. Because we allow Heavenly Father to be in control, we no longer carry the stress of trying to make everything turn out the way we think it should. We simply do our part, do our best, and then hand the outcome over to Heavenly Father. Like all commandments, becoming humble is a real gift, not a bothersome requirement.

Not only is humility a strength in and of itself, humility is also the catalyst for turning other weaknesses into strength. The prophet Moroni recorded this truth when the Lord responded to his concern that his written words would be mocked. Moroni knew the Lord had made him strong in speaking, but perceived his writing as a weakness.[5] This was part of the Lord's response: "And if men come unto me I will show unto them their weakness. I give unto men weakness that they may be humble; and my grace is sufficient for all men that humble themselves before me; for if they humble themselves before me, and have faith in me, then will I make weak things become strong unto them."[6] Isn't that wonderful? When we view our weaknesses as stepping stones to humility, and difficulties that will someday actually become strengths, it spins everything into a brand new picture. It makes discouragement dissipate and creates a feeling of anticipation and excitement as we prepare to use the strengthening and enabling power of the Atonement to change. Elder David A. Bednar taught, "Individual willpower, personal determination and motivation, effective planning and goal setting are necessary but ultimately insufficient for us to triumphantly complete this mortal journey. Truly, we must come to rely upon 'the merits, and mercy, and grace of the Holy Messiah' (2 Nephi 2:8)."[7] This article, which was originally presented to students at a Brigham Young University Devotional, enlightens us about effectively accepting and using the Atonement for more than just forgiveness of sins. He instructs us to make a habit of not just being good, but becoming *better* as we rely on the Atonement. We must remember that the purpose of mortality is to gain experience that will lead us into eternal life. This can only happen by the grace of God (or enabling power of the Atonement)[8] – while doing our part. "Becoming" is a continual action. It requires daily effort. Elder Jorg Klebingat shared six steps that, if put into practice, will allow us to be spiritually confident in the presence of God. Every one of those steps requires consistent, daily work. He said, "Spiritual confidence increases when you take responsibility for your own spiritual well-being by applying the Atonement of Jesus Christ daily ... Spiritual confidence increases when your spirit, with the help of the Savior, is truly in charge of your natural man or woman."[9] When using the Atonement properly, our natures are changed, our weaknesses become strengths, our confidence increases, and humility becomes part of who we are. As we are working to eliminate weaknesses by humbling ourselves and coming to the Lord for help, it is good for us to remember that it really is only through Him that we can change. Elder M. Russell Ballard spoke of repairing the "chinks in our armor" as we are

39

seeking to protect ourselves from evil. "…Reach out and humble yourself. The Lord's enabling power is sufficient to change your heart, to turn your life, to purge your soul. But you must make the first move, which is to humble yourself and realize that only in God can you find deliverance."[10] It is humility which helps us to recognize that we cannot change alone. Changing our natures from fallen to exalted requires humble use of the Atonement. When King Benjamin called his people together for his final address to them, he taught the truths of the Plan of Salvation.[11] When he was finished, "he sent among them, desiring to know of his people if they believed the words which he had spoken unto them. And they all cried with one voice, saying: Yea, we believe all the words which thou hast spoken unto us; and also we know of their surety and truth, because of the Spirit of the Lord Omnipotent, which has wrought a *mighty change* in us, or in our hearts, that we have no more disposition to do evil, but to do good continually."[12] This mighty change is the enabling and strengthening power of the Atonement working in their lives, as it can work in ours. This is what grace is. By tapping into the Atonement, we can recognize our weaknesses as a means to nurture humility in our lives. As we do so, we develop strengths – which are really gifts bestowed by our Father – that will help us move forward on our mortal journey toward our eternal futures.

I love the visual picture created by the beginning of this phrase: "… they did *wax* stronger and stronger in their humility …" Of course, the meaning of the word "wax" in this instance is to increase or grow. But picture candle making: One begins the process by melting wax, then holding a sizeable amount of wick in the hand. After dipping the wick into the wax, the wick is barely coated. When pulling the wick out of the wax the first time, there is no recognizable shape to the candle – it's not straight, it's all wiggly, having gotten wet and being bent here and there by the quickly hardening first layer of wax. The process of creating a usable candle (or even just a pretty one) requires patience and consistent dipping. Dipping the wick just one time and holding it in the wax longer *will not* create a thicker coat. It is required to pull the wick out and let the wax harden after each dip so the wax can build on each previous layer, thus creating a candle. When a coat of wax becomes hard enough to withstand a dip back into the hot liquid, it serves as a steady frame for the next coat to add to. Eventually, after dipping, cooling and hardening, then repeating over and over, a candle is created. The candle then provides light and heat in this way: "When you light a candle, the heat of the flame melts the wax near the wick. This liquid wax is then drawn up the wick by capillary action. The heat of the flame vaporizes the liquid wax (turns it into a hot gas), and starts to break down the hydrocarbons into molecules of hydrogen and carbon. These vaporized molecules are drawn up into the flame, where they react with oxygen from the air to create heat, light, water vapor (H_2O) and carbon dioxide (CO_2). Approximately one-fourth of the energy created by a candle's combustion is given off as heat radiates from the flame in all directions. Enough heat is created to radiate back and melt more wax to keep the combustion process going until the fuel is used up or the heat is eliminated."[13] So the more times the candle was dipped in wax, the longer it will be able to provide light and heat.

It's an interesting way to consider growing our humility. When we begin our journey to intentionally become humble, our first few "dips in the wax" will not create a candle. In other words, the situation that is providing us an opportunity to become humble will not immediately rid us of pride and fill us with humility. But it's a beginning. When we emerge the first few times from our "dips" we may be a little out of shape and uncomfortable. But as we let those dips do their work (like the wax on a wick cooling and hardening) we will be prepared for the next dip. And the next. The more we work on humility the stronger we become. Pretty soon, we've waxed so strong that we're prepared to give light and warmth to those around us.

While exploring the word "wax" I was taught that its origin is Anglo-Saxon. But they also had a word similar in sound, "weaxan" which meant "to increase." The root for this word evolved into Greek as "auxein" – meaning "augment." This is interesting because one of the definitions for the word augment is "swell." When we consider our humility as something that swells, the picture that creates for me is pushing other things away. When humility swells within us, the characteristics and effects of pride are pushed out of ourselves. There is no more room for criticism, selfishness, backbiting, or envying. We stop obsessing about ourselves, stop trying to compete with our neighbors, and stop withholding gratitude or forgiveness. As humility swells within us we "have no more disposition to do evil, but to do good continually."[14] The Atonement becomes a continual force for change. The swelling of humility leaves no room for self-pity, self-absorption, self-aggrandizement. Instead we become filled with charity and our focus becomes others. We become truly happy.

I was blessed to be with my parents during a time when my mother was not strong enough to attend Sacrament Meeting. I stayed home with her, and later that afternoon two Priesthood holders came to my parents' house with the sacrament. It was one of the most tender sacrament experiences I've had. I've visited my parents often enough that I know many of their ward members. But one of the Priesthood holders who was in their home that day was not familiar to me. After the administration of the sacrament we visited for a bit. I learned that the unfamiliar brother was just beginning activity back in the church after a twenty year absence. As he spoke with us, his face was illuminated with a real happiness. He shared his feelings that he was the one being blessed with the opportunity to serve. This brother exhibited true humility as he left the comfort of his home, late on a Sunday, and knelt in the family room of a person who didn't want to miss the opportunity to partake of the sacrament. I don't know much about this brother's journey, but I do know that stepping out to serve was a "dip in the wax" and that he was truly happy as he was focused on serving.

When we are "waxing stronger and stronger in humility" that may mean we have graduated past being "compelled to be humble."[15] We will recognize not only our own nothingness, but also our divinity. "Ironically, our blindness toward our human weaknesses will also make us blind to the divine potential that our Father yearns to nurture within each of us."[16] As we intentionally work to grow our humility, true joy fills our beings and we can then see life – it's splendor and its hardship - with proper perspective. We stop complaining and comparing because we recognize each moment of life as an opportunity for growth and joy. Like the people of Helaman's time, it won't matter what our peers think of us, how others treat us, what hardship comes our way. We'll continue to live with prayerful hearts, focus our minds and actions on serving others, and see the good in life.

[1] Dictionary.com, Pride

[2] LDS General Conference, April 1989, Beware of Pride, Ezra Taft Benson

[3] LDS General Conference, October 2010, Pride and the Priesthood, Dieter F. Uchtdorf

[4] Doctrine and Covenants 42:45

[5] The Book of Mormon, Ether 12:25

[6] The Book of Mormon, Ether 12:27

[7] Ensign Magazine, April 2012, The Atonement and the Journey of Mortality, David A. Bednar

[8] Bible Dictionary page 697, Grace

[9] LDS General Conference, October 2014, Approaching the Throne of God with Confidence, Jorg Klebingat

[10] LDS Church Educational Fireside, March 3, 2002, Be Strong in The Lord, M. Russell Ballard

[11] The Book of Mormon, Mosiah 2-5

[12] The Book of Mormon, Mosiah 5:1-2 (italics added)

[13] Candles.org, How Candles Burn

[14] The Book of Mormon, Mosiah 5:2

[15] LDS General Conference, April 1989, Beware of Pride, Ezra Taft Benson

[16] LDS General Conference, October 2014, Lord is it I?, Dieter F. Uchtdorf

AND FIRMER AND FIRMER IN THE FAITH OF CHRIST

"Faith in Jesus Christ is a gift from heaven that comes as we choose to believe and as we seek it and hold on to it. Your faith is either growing stronger or becoming weaker," spoke Elder Neil L. Andersen.[1] The people of Helaman's time were making a clear choice to increase their faith. They did this through regular fasting, prayer, service and humbly working toward becoming more righteous. As Elder Andersen taught, it takes work on our part to have faith. The fact that Helaman's people waxed "firmer and firmer in the faith of Christ" tells us that they worked at it. They didn't have perfect faith just handed to them, and that's what kept them going! Rather, they chose to believe and focused on growing their belief into firm faith. In part, it was the work of growing faith that kept them going. Instead of focusing on how persecuted and hated they were, they focused on being better people.

We know that faith is a principle of action.[2] Otherwise, it's just belief. Faith grows as we practice, as we exercise it. The Prophet Joseph Smith not only believed that God gives answers to heartfelt prayers, but he also had the faith to act.[3] In referring to the New Testament scripture verses[4] that prompted the boy Joseph to act on his faith, Elder David A. Bednar said, "Please notice the requirement to ask in faith, which I understand to mean the necessity to not only express but to do, the dual obligation to both plead and to perform, the requirement to communicate and to act."[5]

Consider the following experiences where, regardless of age and life experience, these people acted on their faith:

He watched with wonder, the kind only a child can have, as his ladybug crawled in and out of his fingers and over his hand. Suddenly, without warning - - - she was gone! He searched and searched, but his Ladybug was nowhere to be found. Then he remembered. His chubby little 3 year old legs took him over to his swing set. He knelt down beside it; folding his arms he rested them on a swing - and prayed. When he opened his eyes there she was, waiting to crawl back onto his hand.

He was a Freshman at college, a newly ordained Elder. A phone call came asking that he and his Home Teaching Companion administer to a young woman who was ill. They rushed to her Dorm, but then doubt and fear surfaced. He was shaking - could he do it? Then he remembered. He excused himself, went into another room and prayed, then returned and pronounced the Lord's blessing upon her. He had found his Ladybug.

He was alone in the Hospital room with his Father. All of his family had been called to travel great distances to see their Dad one more time, as he was near death. He felt prompted to pronounce a blessing, promising his father full recovery - - - No. He shouldn't take that upon himself, he must wait for a brother to arrive, and also ask his Mother who should seal the anointing. The next morning, as he and his brothers gave their father yet another blessing, he was able to pronounce the Lord's promise upon their Father - - - full recovery. He had found his Ladybug.[6]

Early each spring our family would order in a shipment of day-old-ducklings. It was an exciting day when our postmaster would call saying they had a box marked "live" and lots of little chirping noises were coming from it! This particular spring we'd ordered all mallards. We already had Donald & Daisy in a big pen – Daisy was sitting on eggs and Donald was keeping a vigilant watch. We didn't know how long it would be till the eggs hatched, and didn't even know if Daisy would let us near. So when our new ducklings arrived they got all our attention. We spent the day giving them each their first drinks of water and watching them toddle around in our "fairy patch." Imagining we could really tell them apart we divided them up and named them. When they got a couple of weeks older, knowing Daisy would soon have little ones hatching, we started giving our ducklings away. But we kept three. Bryan, Sierra and Azure each kept one duckling to raise. We had to keep the little ones away from Donald & Daisy. Daisy was very protective of her eggs and wouldn't let a soul – duckling or human – near. So the babies had their own little cage. We lived in Southeast Alaska where predators are prolific. Among the most dangerous to ducklings in early spring are bald eagles. Before the herring spawn, there's not a whole lot for them to eat and a baby duck looks mighty tasty. So we'd cover their little wooden home with fishing net to keep the eagles away.

One morning, before the noise of the day, I was awakened to crazy quacking. I recognized it was Daisy – screaming as it were. I ran out the front door to Daisy's cage to see what horror was causing her alarm. Sure that she just wanted Donald out of the cage, I was a little put out to be awakened so rudely. When I saw Daisy off the eggs and quacking, not at Donald, but at the world, I opened her cage to let her out. As she ran right past me, I turned to see what could be disturbing her so much. To my horror I saw a giant river otter slither up and out of the ducklings' cage. I'm not sure the words I used, but I remember calling to my husband to hurry and come. Daisy and I chased the otter, who was faster than one can imagine on his stubby legs. Daisy didn't stop chasing and quacking till the otter was so far up the creek he was no longer visible. Brad and I were sickened as we looked inside the ducklings' cage to see all three laying still. Then there was movement – ever so slight. One was still alive. It was Gracie, Sierra's duck. But she was in bad shape. Her head had been crushed and she was losing an eye. As Brad reached down with a cloth to wipe some of the blood off, she twitched and froze. Gracie should have been dead. When the kids heard about the attack, their first response was to gather for prayer. Brad and I were prepared to help end Gracie's pain and to bury her with the others, but the kids would hear none of that. There was no reason Gracie could not recover, they told us. Her sight could come back, it's possible she could have normal brain function ... So we prayed. All of us. We prayed a lot. We kept Gracie warm with a heat lamp and a towel. Day after day Sierra nursed Gracie back to health, spending her days by her side and taking her safely into the garage at night. Eventually Gracie started to sip water. Then as Sierra would force a little food into her mouth, Gracie would make an effort to swallow. Much to our delight, Gracie fought for life. Finally, Gracie's strength started to return. She got up and started to waddle. And then she was interested in food again. Sierra took her down to the creek and Gracie's natural actions returned. The kids built a little dam for Gracie – the water pooled and Gracie could safely swim. Bit by bit Gracie's sight started to return on one side and she started acting like a normal duck. Daisy's ducklings hatched, and although Gracie was humanized, she started social interactions with the others. Soon Gracie was just one of the other ducks. Many cool summer evenings Gracie sat in Sierra's lap as we visited outside and watched the other ducks waddle around the yard. Sierra's care and the children's faith gave Gracie back her life.

Madison Elementary School was just across the street and through a field from our home. I was just 6-years-old and in a combined first and second grade class. Mrs. Wadlow was one of those teachers a child idolizes and never forgets. I still have the broken china horse and buggy she let me pick out from her gifts for students one year. The last time I corresponded with Mrs. Wadlow was right before my mission. I sent her a letter telling of my mission call; she sent a congratulations letter. When I returned from my mission I sent her a letter only to have it returned. I suspect she had passed away. Every day in Mrs. Wadlow's class was enjoyable. After school I'd saunter through the field on my way home, often stepping off the path to pick up a horned-toad or examine a lone flower growing in the dry field of dirt. One day on my way home I took in the beauty of a young tree. The leaves seemed to shimmer as the breeze passed by and I found myself wanting to look at the tree forever. Although just a little tree, I knew it was way too big for me to dig it up and take home. So I determined to grow one of my own. Plucking a leaf from this magical looking tree I hurried home to share the good news with my mother. I told her I really, really wanted my own sparkling tree, and asked for a little plot of dirt in our yard to plant it. Mom took me out to the breezeway, handed me a spoon and showed me where to dig. Years later I asked my mom why she didn't tell me that you can't grow a tree from a leaf. Her response: "Who am I to say what can and can't happen with enough faith?" I prayed over that little leaf every day, knowing that it is Heavenly Father who created the leaf, and He would create my new tree. I remember taking a cup of water to the breezeway each day before school to water my leaf. Each day after school, I'd zip home to check on my tree. Every prayer I said included a request for blessings on my tree. One day I was rewarded. A sprout was shooting up right where I had been watering each day. Excitedly, I called to Mom as I ran into the house. My tree was finally growing! I would have my own tree that would glisten in the breezeway! My tree became my project. Daily I'd water the little seedling. Weeks passed, then months. Finally one day the plant started to get leaves of its own.

Much to my mother's amazement, this little plant really was a silver dollar tree! My leaf was now a tree.

Now, more than 40 years later, I sit at the computer reading up on silver dollar trees. While searching the internet for "how to propagate a silver dollar tree" it's clear that one must have a root-cutting for a new tree to grow. I suspect my mother already knew that you must start with a rooted plant … but because of her wisdom and her nurturing spirit, she not only provided the spoon and the plot, but she provided the encouragement and support necessary for a young girl's faith to be exercised and grown.

I was a brand new missionary in Japan. My trainer quickly oriented me and told me about our current investigators. Miwako was scheduled for baptism within a couple of weeks. We also had two other girls as regular investigators. Shindo Shimai (Sister Shindo) and Iwabuchi Shimai (Sister Iwabuchi) were not only best friends, but long time church goers. They had been studying the gospel for 2 years but both sets of parents had refused to give permission for their baptisms. Although they were spiritually fed in their Young Women activities and other church meetings, we continued to meet with them regularly. Two months after arriving in Japan, and after my first companion had transferred, our investigator pool continued to grow. We taught another young woman who was "golden" and was preparing for her baptism later that week. Our regular meeting with Shindo Shimai and Iwabuchi Shimai was a few days before this baptism. Although both of these young sisters were not able to get baptized, they always attended our baptisms and rejoiced with the new converts. This particular meeting, Shindo Shimai expressed great sadness that she wasn't the one getting baptized. I felt prompted to share the following (taken from my journal): *First of all, you must have a lot of faith – really a lot. Please go into your bedroom and pray and tell Heavenly Father how much you want to be baptized. Then write a note that says, "My daughter has my permission to be baptized Saturday, June 21st"* *then pray again that Heavenly Father will really help you, and tell* *him again how much you want to be baptized. Then go to your* *mother, give her the note and ask her to sign it.* I told her that my companion and I would be praying for her too. Well, she did just as I asked her to do. She said that it took her 2 hours and a lot of tears – but her mom finally gave in and signed the paper – a paper she had refused to sign for years.   Her friend, Iwabuchi Shimai didn't feel the same degree of sadness and urgency at that time.   But when I was nearing the end of my mission I was contacted by the mission office and given permission to attend Iwabuchi Shimai's baptism outside of my current area. Iwabuchi Shimai finally felt the same urgency and exerted similar faith and action as her friend did. She received the necessary permission from her parents.

Yes, faith grows as we exercise it by combining sincere prayer with action on our part. As we act on faith in Christ, our foundation gets stronger – our faith becomes firmer and firmer.   In my mind firmness is something tangible. Think of picking out good fruit at the grocery store – we avoid the soft and mushy, bruised and marked fruit. Instead, when we pick up an apple or other fruit we give it a little squeeze to test its firmness. If it passes the test it goes in the bag. How firm is our faith? When we give it a little squeeze, does it hold up? Does it pass the test?

When Helaman died, the judgment seat was given to his oldest son, Nephi. The Nephites became more and more prideful, more and more wicked. So much so, that when dissenters gathered forces with the Lamanites, the Nephites lost many battles.   The wickedness of his people weighed so heavily on Nephi that he gave up the judgment seat. He and his brother Lehi made the choice to spend the rest of their lives preaching, with the hopes of bringing as many as possible to God. As they began their missionary work, the words   their   father   had   taught   them   offered   strength, encouragement, and resolve: "And now, my sons, remember, remember that it is upon the rock of our Redeemer, who is Christ, the Son of God, that ye must build your foundation; that when the devil shall send forth his mighty winds, yea, his shafts in the whirlwind, yea, when all his hail and his mighty storm shall beat upon you, it shall have no power over you to drag you down to the gulf of misery and endless wo, because of the rock upon which ye are built, which is a sure foundation, a foundation whereon if men build they cannot fall."[7] Firmness is required in any foundation. When Christ is our foundation, it doesn't matter what comes our way, we will continue to stand. This is because Christ will never leave us! He is always there to strengthen us, comfort us, guide us, and direct us. We sing of this foundation in our meetings:

> How firm a foundation, ye Saints of the Lord,
> Is laid for your faith in his excellent word!
> What more can he say than to you he hath said,
> Who unto the Savior for refuge have fled?
>
> In every condition – in sickness, in health,
> In poverty's vale or abounding in wealth,
> At home or abroad, on the land or the sea
> As thy days may demand so thy succor shall be.
>
> Fear not, I am with thee; oh, be not dismayed,
> For I am thy God and will still give thee aid.
> I'll strengthen thee, help thee, and cause thee to stand,
> Upheld by my righteous, omnipotent hand.
>
> When through the deep waters I call thee to go,
> The rivers of sorrow shall not thee o'erflow,
> For I will be with thee, thy troubles to bless,
> And sanctify to thee thy deepest distress.

When through fiery trials thy pathway shall lie,
My grace, all sufficient, shall be thy supply.
Thy flame shall not hurt thee; I only design
Thy dross to consume and thy gold to refine.

E'en down to old age, all my people shall prove
My sovereign, eternal, unchangeable love;
And then, when gray hair shall their temples adorn,
Like lambs shall they still in my bosom be borne.

The soul that on Jesus hath leaned for repose
I will not, I cannot, desert to his foes;
That soul, though all hell should endeavor to shake,
I'll never, no never, no never forsake![8]

It is required that our faith be in our Savior, Jesus Christ. And it is required that we grow our faith – so that it gets firmer and firmer. Otherwise it will weaken. The great news is that we get to start where we are today! We don't need to be concerned if our faith has been a little mushy – not really very firm – in the past. We get to concentrate on firming it up, starting with today. "Begin exercising your faith in every area of your life. If you don't, you will suffer what I would call 'faith atrophy.' The very strength needed to exercise your faith will be diminished. So exercise your faith every day," stated Elder Robert D. Hales.[9] Every day! It's true that each and every day there are opportunities to grow our faith. As we experiment on this, we may be surprised at the simple things we've already been doing that have us headed in the right direction. Some of these may include: Praying; choosing to be happy even on a gloomy day; setting a goal; helping someone in need. These, and many other things we do throughout a regular day, are acts of faith. Taking these actions helps our faith become firmer and firmer.

I find it interesting that the people in Helaman's time who were being persecuted by their more affluent peers received greater faith – not release from the persecution. They aren't the only people who have prayed and acted in faith but have still had to carry their burdens. The scriptures are full of people who have been in horrible circumstances – when they prayed in faith, their circumstances didn't change, but they were made strong and able to rise above the hardship. Elder David A. Bednar shared an experience of one Mormon Pioneer whose faith in Christ was firm. When he prayed through a hardship, he prayed to be strengthened:

Daniel W. Jones was born in 1830 in Missouri, and he joined the Church in California in 1851. In 1856 he participated in the rescue of handcart companies that were stranded in Wyoming by severe snowstorms. After the rescue party had found the suffering Saints, provided what immediate comfort they could, and made arrangements for the sick and the feeble to be transported to Salt Lake City, Daniel and several other young men volunteered to remain with and safeguard the company's possessions. The food and supplies left with Daniel and his colleagues were meager and rapidly expended. The following quote from Daniel Jones's personal journal describes the events that followed. "Game soon became so scarce that we could kill nothing. We ate all the poor meat; one would get hungry eating it. Finally that was all gone, nothing now but hides were left. We made a trial of them. A lot was cooked and eaten without any seasoning and it made the whole company sick. … Things looked dark, for nothing remained but the poor raw hides taken from starved cattle. We asked the Lord to direct us what to do. The brethren did not murmur, but felt to trust in God. … Finally I was impressed how to fix the stuff and gave the company advice, telling them how to cook it; for them to scorch and scrape the hair off; this had a tendency to kill and purify the bad taste that scalding gave it. After scraping, boil one hour in plenty of water, throwing the water away which had extracted all the glue, then wash and scrape the hide thoroughly, washing in cold water, then boil to a jelly and let it get cold, and then eat with a little sugar sprinkled on it. This was considerable trouble, but we had little else to do and it was better than starving. We asked the Lord to bless our stomachs and adapt them to this food. ... On eating now all seemed to relish the feast. We were three days without eating before this second attempt was made. We enjoyed this sumptuous fare for about six weeks."[10]

Like Helaman's people, Daniel Jones had faith when hardship hit him ... and then his faith became firmer and firmer as he prayed and acted. Faith in Christ doesn't mean that we expect Him to make our troubles go away. It means that we trust that He will guide us, direct us, and lift us. We believe that He is by our side and will strengthen us. Our faith will become firmer and firmer as we focus on the Savior. We promise weekly, as we partake of the sacrament, to "always remember Him."[11] When Christ is in our thoughts it will be natural for us to grasp every opportunity to grow our faith. We will not shrink from it, we won't choose the easy way when faced with hardship. Like Daniel Jones, we will pray for strength and then we will act.

[1] LDS General Conference, October 2015, Faith Is Not By Chance, But By Choice, Neil L. Andersen

[2] Lectures on Faith 1:9, Joseph Smith

[3] Pearl of Great Price, Joseph Smith History

[4] The New Testament, James 1:5-6

[5] LDS General Conference, April 2008, Ask In Faith, David A. Bednar

[6] Michael D. Call Personal Experience – Used with permission

[7] The Book of Mormon, Helaman 5:12

[8] LDS Hymnbook #85

[9] LDS General Conference, October 2015, Meeting the Challenges of Today's World, Robert D. Hales

[10] Ensign Magazine, April 2012, The Atonement and the Journey of Mortality, David A. Bednar

[11] The Book of Mormon, Moroni 4:3

UNTO THE FILLING THEIR SOULS WITH JOY AND CONSOLATION

It was fasting and praying regularly, becoming humble by loving God and their fellow men, and increasing their faith even in the midst of hardship, that filled Helaman's people's souls with joy and consolation. Elder Daniel P. Alvarez told us that "joy is a condition of great happiness, which is the result of righteous living."[1] We know that Helaman's people were living righteously – that is the very reason that they were being persecuted. But righteousness isn't a one-time achievement. As we've discussed in earlier chapters, it's a constant progression. And interestingly, the more righteous we become, the more we learn about things we need to change, in order to become even better. Righteousness is a progressive state. It is fluid, not stagnant. If we want joy, we need to be happy. Happiness comes as we live righteously, to the degree which we then understand, and as we participate in "ongoing, joyful, happy repentance."[2]

When I was four or five years old I had an experience of repentance which has stuck with me. My older sister had gone on a trip to visit relatives. I think it was her first time being away from home alone. While on this trip she and the cousins she was with visited Disneyland. I missed her terribly while she was gone, but she had promised to bring a present from Disneyland, so I decided it was ok that she left. While she was gone I made a present for her. I carefully gathered the prettiest colors of tissue paper I could find, then searched for tape and glue. When it was all gathered I created a paper folder for her. I thought it would be perfect for her to keep her school work in. The outside was decorated with paper flowers – but as I think back on it now, there was a lot more tape than paper. Still, I was proud of the gift I'd present to her upon her return. I created the folder within the first couple of days of Camielle's being gone, and so I really anticipated her return. I was nearly as excited to give her the present as I was to receive whatever it was she was bringing to me. Well, finally the day arrived. Camielle was coming home. Within minutes of stepping into the house Camielle said or did something to upset me. I can't recall what it was, but I was so upset that I ran into the bedroom, snatched up the paper folder that I had put my whole heart into, and ripped it into a few pieces. I stuffed it under the bed and with tear-filled eyes emerged from the room. I don't think any member of the family had a clue that I was so upset, nor did they know how I had acted out. I was angry. I had stopped thinking about anyone but myself – I couldn't understand how everyone could be so happy. The family was gathered together, just waiting for me to join them, and Camielle had her suitcase opened in front of her. She was ready to give out presents. I was still seething and feeling justified in destroying the gift I had for Camielle when she pulled my present out of the suitcase. She'd gotten little dolls for me ... The Seven Dwarfs. I couldn't believe she would give me something so wonderful! I held out my hands to receive the dolls, then broke into tears and ran back into my room. I didn't deserve something this nice! I had been so bad! I was very young, but I knew that my heart was not right. I knelt by my bed and prayed to be forgiven. While in the attitude of repentance I hurriedly searched for the tape and repaired the folder the very best that I could. I knew that true repentance meant making things right again. I didn't have time to create an entirely new folder, and besides – I doubted I could ever make one as nice as the first one. So I taped it together and ran out of the room, the folder behind my back. "I made something for you, Camielle." I had her close her eyes and hold out her hands. She barely had time to see what I gave her before I reached both arms around her and hugged tightly. I began to cry and told her how sorry I was that I'd ruined her present. Certainly, I'd had circumstances to apologize before that in my life, and many, many times after that. But I remember that experience as a time when my heart was truly broken. My spirit was contrite. I repented fully and completely. I was happy again. "Joy is much deeper than simply passing moments of contentment or feelings of happiness. Real joy, or 'everlasting joy'[3]comes from experiencing the power of the Atonement through sincere repentance and from a spiritual confirmation that we can be redeemed from sin through the Lord Jesus Christ and inherit eternal life."[4]

As children we were exposed to happiness daily as our mother would sing throughout the day. She'd sing in the kitchen while preparing meals, in the car on our way to and from places, and pretty much all day regardless of what was going on. Our father would sing in the morning as he'd walk into our rooms to wake us. "Oh what a beautiful morning, Oh what a beautiful day! I have a beautiful feeling everything's going my way!"[5] Through song we learned that our circumstances couldn't make us happy or sad – we *choose* happy or sad. Two of the songs that were sung regularly by my mom reinforced that truth. We would often join in as Mom sang:

"Be happy," sings the little bird
On boughs beneath the blue;
Be happy, happy all day long,
And others will be too!

"Be happy," trills the little brook
While running meadows through;
Be happy, happy all day long,
And others will be too!

"Be happy," shouts the wind of morn,
As o'er the land it flied;
"Be happy," south winds whisper low,
And every wave replies,

Be happy all day long
Each day you'll find it true;
That he whose heart has joy and song
Gives joy to others too.[6]

But my favorite, and one that I sang often as our children were growing up was:

I am happy today for the sunshine,
For the skies of gray or blue;
For within my heart is a song of joy:
I'll live, I'll work, I'll do.

No cloud can cast a shadow
Over courage such as mine.
And I'll sing my song as I go along:
I'll live, I'll work, I'll do![7]

The truth that we learned as children, and that the people of Helaman well knew, is that it really doesn't matter what's going on in the world, at work, or even among people we're close to. It's our choice to be happy and thus experience joy.

It also doesn't matter where we are on the road of progression, but rather the direction we're headed. Whether the repentance required for us to maintain true joy is as simple as taping together a paper folder, or as deep as confessing and forsaking addicting habits, daily work is required. Brigham Young said, "The men and women who desire to obtain seats in the celestial kingdom will find that they must battle every day."[8] Knowing that it's the direction we're headed rather than exactly where we are on the path gives me great comfort. I'm reminded of Alma the Younger and his friends, the sons of Helaman. We know the good that these righteous men did as missionaries. They brought thousands to God. But sometimes we forget that before their conversions, before their missionary experiences, "they were the very vilest of sinners."[9] Their repentance process wasn't easy, but they did it. I'm certain that these men repented daily – even after their conversion while they were on the Lord's errand as missionaries. It is because of this progressive righteous behavior that they were able to experience incredible joy. While out working hard to bring others to eternal happiness, these men met up with each other: "And it came to pass that as Ammon was going forth into the land, that he and his brethren met Alma, over in the place of which has been spoken; and behold, this was a *joyful* meeting. Now the *joy* of Ammon was so great even that he was full; yea, he was swallowed up in the *joy* of his God, even to the exhausting of his strength; and he fell again to the earth. Now was not this exceeding *joy*? Behold, this is *joy* which none receiveth save it be the *truly penitent and humble seeker of happiness.*"[10] These men sought happiness. They did it with humility and with honest, regular repentance. Certainly they fasted and prayed often, just as the people of Helaman did.

It is interesting that not only were Helaman's people *filled* with joy and consolation, but Ammon (who fell to the Earth because of his exceeding joy) was also *filled*. When completely filled, it means there is no room for anything else. There's no room for pride or anger; no room for hurt, backbiting, self-pity, or comparisons. Being filled means being filled. How wonderful to be filled with joy and with consolation! And it wasn't just their minds or their hearts that were filled ... it was their *souls*. That's everything! "And the spirit and the body are the soul of man."[11] To have our spirits and our bodies *filled* with joy and consolation is a gift, indeed! The

Ancient American prophet, Lehi, shared his vision of the tree of life with his family: "And it came to pass that I beheld a tree, whose fruit was desirable to make one happy. And it came to pass that I did go forth and partake of the fruit thereof; and I beheld that it was most sweet, above all that I ever before tasted. Yea, and I beheld that the fruit thereof was white, to exceed all the whiteness that I had ever seen. And as I partook of the fruit thereof it *filled my soul with exceedingly great joy*; wherefore, I began to be desirous that my family should partake of it also."[12] Later, Lehi's son, Nephi, desired to know the interpretation of the dream and the meaning of the fruit of the tree of life. "... it is the love of God, which sheddeth itself abroad in the hearts of the children of men; wherefore, it is the most desirable above all things. And he spake unto me, saying: Yea, and the *most joyous to the soul*."[13] The people of Helaman were able to be filled with the love of God because they were making daily righteous choices.

This was a trying time for Helaman's people. We are in trying times now. Whether looking at the condition the world is in, or at our personal lives – we are consistently being tried. Sometimes the trials create great heartache and hurt. Sometimes great concern. But following the example of the righteous people who withstood persecution and continued in fasting, prayer, service and humility, will create the same joy and consolation for us that they received. Did they need to be comforted and consoled? Surely they did! The people they had associated with throughout their lives were turning on them. They were ridiculing them and hurting them. Likely there were family members and close friends who had turned against them. If anyone was in need of consolation, surely they were. How tender that the Lord not only filled them with joy, but also with consolation. We know that as we live worthily we can have the Holy Ghost, who is the Comforter, as our constant companion. We can receive comfort and consolation as we plead for it. We know that as we reach out and serve other people, thinking more of others than we do of ourselves, our own troubles diminish. But I also believe that much of the comfort and consolation came from *receiving* service. Certainly those being persecuted served each other and did what they could to lift each others' burdens. Both those who served and those who received were blessed with joy and consolation.

My parents were just in their 50s when, while traveling far from home, my father was taken by ambulance and admitted to a hospital with a brain hemorrhage. It was so serious that family members were called from all over the world to say their good-byes. Our mother was strengthened by having all her children near, but her heart hurt knowing that any moment could be her last with her husband in mortality. The injury took place in a state far from home. There were no friends or family near to help lift the burdens. But there were good people, strangers, who reached out offering a place to do laundry, food to eat, and prayers in the family's behalf. All of us fasted and prayed often. We were comforted. Much of the consolation our mother received was from mortal angels who were "willing to bear one another's burdens, that they may be light; Yea, and...willing to mourn with those that mourn; yea, and comfort those that stand in need of comfort..."[14] Some of these people were themselves hurting, as they were family members of other patients. Yet they reached out in service and comfort to us. Some were covenant making and covenant keeping people who made sure our family was able to take the sacrament. Some were good medical professionals who recognized the power of prayer that strengthened them as they did their work to help our father. Our mother, and all of us, received joy and consolation during a time that was truly trying. We received that, not only because we were trying to live righteously, but because others were too.

In reference to Helaman's people, Elder Gerald Lund said, "Isn't that something we all seek ... to be visited by the Holy Ghost, to have the Lord draw closer to us, to find *joy and consolation* in our lives? If so, then carefully assessing the condition of our hearts is one of the most essential things we can do in this life."[15] When our hearts are open and softened, we are then able to see what the Lord wants us to see. Our perspective changes. We begin to view mortality as part of eternity. We see that our circumstances don't have to be stumbling blocks, but can be stepping stones for progression. When our hearts are open and soft, we don't take offense easily; we learn to love those who may not love us. "The nearer we get to our Heavenly Father, the more we are disposed to look with compassion on perishing souls: we feel that we want to take them upon our shoulders, and cast their sins behind our backs,"[16] stated the Prophet Joseph Smith. There are many examples in the scriptures of those who, because their hearts were soft, honestly sought for the eternal welfare of those who were considered their enemies. Alma and the sons of Mosiah were some who left comfortable situations to preach to their enemies.[17] Enos prayed through the night for a remission of sins, then continued to pray for his brethren, and finally, for his enemies.[18] Samuel the Lamanite,[19] Abinadi the prophet,[20] and Nephi and Lehi,[21] the sons of Helaman, reached out to share the saving truths of the Gospel with those who wished them dead. All of these people experienced the mighty change of heart[22] often enough to keep their hearts soft and open. This resulted in joy and consolation when they needed it. "Why the heart? Because the heart is a synonym for one's entire makeup. The measure of our hearts is the measure of our total performance. As used by the Lord, the heart of a person describes his effort to better self, or others, or the conditions he confronts."[23] And so, when we do as Elder Lund suggested and carefully assess the condition of our hearts on a daily basis, we will be more likely to make necessary changes. We will be more able to see our own imperfections rather than other people's. When assessing our heart daily we will be more open to the Spirit and thus open to receiving joy and consolation, which will push out negative feelings. When assessing the heart regularly, we will be likely to "always retain a remission of...sins." Additionally, we will "always rejoice, and be filled with the love of God."[24] Like the people of Helaman's time, our *entire souls* will be *filled* with joy and consolation!

[1] LDS General Conference, April 2006, The Sweet Peace of Forgiveness, Daniel P. Alvarez

[2] LDS General Conference, October 2014, Approaching the Throne of God with Confidence, Jorg Klebingat

[3] The Book of Mormon, 2 Nephi 8:11

[4] LDS General Conference, April 2007, Lessons from The New Testament: The Joy of Repentance, Craig C. Christensen

[5] Oscar Hammerstein, "Oh What a Beautiful Morning"

[6] The Children Sing, No.94 Be Happy

[7] Source Unknown

[8] Discourses of Brigham Young, Page 392, Salt Lake City: Deseret Book, 1954

[9] The Book of Mormon, Mosiah 28:4

[10] The Book of Mormon, Alma 27:16-18 (italics added)

[11] Doctrine and Covenants 88:15

[12] The Book of Mormon, 1 Nephi 8:10-12 (italics added)

[13] The Book of Mormon, 1 Nephi 11:22-23 (italics added)

[14] The Book of Mormon, Mosiah 18:8-9

[15] LDS General Conference, April 2008, Opening our Hearts, Gerald N. Lund (italics added)

[16] Teachings of the Prophet Joseph Smith, Page 241

[17] The Book of Mormon, Alma 17-26

[18] The Book of Mormon, Enos 1

[19] The Book of Mormon, Helaman 13-15

[20] The Book of Mormon, Mosiah 11-17

[21] The Book of Mormon, Helaman 5-7

[22] The Book of Mormon, Alma 5:14

[23] LDS General Conference, October 1988, The Measure of Our Hearts, Marvin J. Ashton

[24] The Book of Mormon, Mosiah 4:12

YEA, EVEN TO THE PURIFYING AND THE SANCTIFICATION OF THEIR HEARTS

The righteous people of Helaman's time not only received joy and consolation (which is really peace) but also had their hearts purified and sanctified! That's how great the effect was of their regular fasting and praying, their loving and serving, and their exercising faith. To purify is to "free from anything that debases, pollutes, adulterates or contaminates."[1] To sanctify is to "make holy, to set apart as sacred."[2] Helaman's people had their hearts both purified and sanctified. It's important to note that this cleansing and being made holy came *after* trials that put them on a path wherein they chose to make righteous decisions and to take righteous actions.

To expect to be purified and sanctified without opposition in our lives is folly. It is exactly *because of* opposition (hardship, trials, adversity) that we are able to become pure and holy. Without opposition we would have no forward motion, we would build no strength, we would not progress. To expect to be purified and sanctified after successfully navigating one big trial is also folly. I can remember thinking at one point in my relatively young life that I had endured enough. I recounted in my mind the many trials I'd had and I decided that it was enough – I was ready for an easy life now. I'd paid the price. It was good enough. Reaching the point of purification and sanctification takes consistent effort. And we are not the ones to decide when it is enough. The people of Helaman's time weren't telling the Lord that they had done their part and were finished with trials – they just kept working at it. They continued to fast and to pray, to grow their faith and to become humble.

The apostle, Paul, is a magnificent example of one who understood exactly what the people of Helaman understood. In fact, Paul (who was beaten, stoned, imprisoned and attacked by Satan) shared his knowledge and his deep testimony of the Savior and also of the purpose of mortality: "Therefore I take pleasure in infirmities, in reproaches, in necessities, in persecutions, in distresses for Christ's sake; for when I am weak, then am I strong."[3]

When thinking about those who endure trials well, one can't help being drawn to the Old Testament prophet, Job. He was stripped of his lifestyle, his health, his comforts, and even his family and friends. Everything was taken from him. But his testimony stayed firm. Surely his heart was purified and sanctified. "[God] knoweth the way that I take: when he hath tried me, I shall come forth as gold. ... His way have I kept, and not declined."[4]

We accepted the gift of mortality, and although we couldn't know exactly how hard it would be, we knew it would be a time of testing and trying. "For behold, this life is the time for men to prepare to meet God; yea, behold the day of this life is the day for men to perform their labors."[5] Adversity comes to us either in the Lord's timing or as a result of mortality. We don't choose when or how it comes to us. Instead of trying to control our circumstances, it's our job to "endure it well."[6] When we're able to remember the purpose of hardship, somehow it becomes easier to bear. We are then able to feel joy and consolation even in the midst of our trials. "We came to mortal life to encounter resistance. It was part of the plan for our eternal progress. Without temptation, sickness, pain, and sorrow, there could be no goodness, virtue, appreciation for well-being, or joy."[7]

I'm not a natural lover of running, but at one point in my life I set a goal to run a marathon. The training plan I chose to follow started out very slowly. It was a 6-month agenda. I began by jogging for a half hour, three days a week and walking two days a week. Bit by bit I stretched myself as the distance and time required to stay on schedule increased. Even though it was a gradual increase it was still very hard for me. About half-way through the training I got plantar fasciitis, which is a painful condition that affects the bottom of the foot. It was related to a weakened arch. I didn't want to stop running and get off the training schedule because I was afraid I would never meet my goal if I did so. I did a lot of reading and researching, talking with professionals and figuring out what would work best for me. In the end, I decided that I would rather work to strengthen my arch than take the stress off my arch and let it heal by artificially supporting it. It was the right choice for me. I used minimalist running shoes and took great care to push through that period of time in a way that would help the condition. In the end, I would get through the pain and have an altogether healthier, stronger foot than if I'd chosen to simply stop the pain. I completed my training and I made it through the marathon. Like some other things in my life, as I look back, I'm glad I did it. But I never want to go through that again. It was painful and hard and exhausting. But I learned and grew and became stronger because of it. Glad I did it; glad it's over. That's the way many of our experiences in life are. We can't just get through day one of training and call it good. We can't say "that's enough" and expect to have the best result. We can't stop right in the midst of pain and say I've grown all I need to grow. That doesn't allow purification to take place. We have to keep practicing, keep training, keep pushing through it with our end goal in sight. As we do so, we become much stronger than we ever imagined we'd be. We qualify ourselves for purification.

Several years ago I joined some members of my family to hike to the bottom the Grand Canyon and back up again. It was a lot of hard work, and we all consider it a great accomplishment. When we were on our way back up the canyon the trail we chose was made up of a whole bunch of switchbacks. We started our hike up the mountain early in the morning so it would be cooler. Back and forth, back and forth we went, slowly climbing to higher elevations. It was June, and in the bottom of the Grand Canyon it was hot – even before the sun started baking us. This created great thirst! We chose our return trail because it had a water source along the way. The water source was called Bright Angel Creek and it emptied into the Colorado River at the base of the canyon. The creek was so enticing whenever we'd be close enough to hear or see it running. Compared to the hot air, the creek was nice and cold. I wanted desperately to drink it, but my husband, who is an avid outdoorsman, cautioned me. "Wait," he said, "it needs to be purified." I learned that running water – a creek, a river, and especially a well, will self-purify. Stagnant water never self-purifies. If it's not moving, the contamination just grows and increases. Depending upon the specifications of running water it may need to run seven miles or more without any additional contamination before it is pure enough to drink. There was no way we could know anything about this creek's contamination so Brad insisted on putting it through a man-made purification process. I wasn't thrilled about this because I was thirsty and wanted to drink immediately. It took time for the water to become pure, but when it had completed the process I was free to drink as much as I wanted.

We lived for a time in a small Alaskan town that boasted its own Artesian well. That was boast-worthy because the water was the best around! It not only tasted good (yes, it tasted different than normal tap water!) but health nuts told us it was really good for us to drink. Why was it so good? Because it was pure. The source was mountain snow in a place where the air is so clear that even special moss grows. The moss is nicknamed "Old Man's Beard" and is very temperamental. It grows only in areas where the air is extremely clean and free of pollutants. So the Artesian well water came from clean snow that became even more purified as it traveled down through layers of the Earth and then defied gravity as it spiraled up again through mineral rocks that breathed life into the water. Imagine the energy it would take for a person to travel so low then work to push back up again! I have imagined that – as I hiked the Grand Canyon I wondered in awe at water that makes a similar trek.

For our hearts to become purified, the process is similar. Most of us are not stagnant. We are somewhere on the path moving toward exaltation. Just like running water or an Artesian well, we may work on purification on our own. But often it takes an outside source, an event, a person, or just the normal effects of mortality, to send us through an even deeper purification process. It serves us well to remember that the very event that is exhausting us and acting as a hardship is also purifying us.

It was hard work for us to grow our family. That is, we struggled through infertility and miscarriage. When our third child was placed in our foster care as an adoptable baby, we were thrilled! But eight months later when the parental rights were terminated we were informed that he would be taken from our care and placed in a home with parents of a similar skin color. At the time we were living on the Pacific island of Guam. My parents were serving a mission in Canada. I called my parents to ask for prayers, but was so broken that I could hardly speak. Later, my mother called me back to reassure me that they were praying for us, but to also teach me. She sent me to the scriptures to see that this was an opportunity for me to become stronger and more pure. Of course, I didn't care about any of that at the time! I just wanted my son. The end of the story is that shortly before Bryan turned two we were able to finalize his adoption. But what took place between that phone call with my mom and the news that Bryan was ours,

71

was truly a refining and purifying time. One of the scriptures my mom referred me to was in The Book of Mormon, Ether chapter six. As I read about the Jaredites who willingly boarded their barges, who were tossed about in the depths of the sea, who "cried unto the Lord,"[8] who were brought back to the surface for a break before being buried in the ocean again, and who "did not cease to praise the Lord,"[9] I understood that although what I was experiencing was hard (really hard) the Lord was mindful of me. I learned that, just like the Jaredites whose journey was successful *because* "the wind did never cease to blow towards the promised land while they were upon the waters; and thus they were driven forth before the wind,"[10] I would also be successful *because of* this trial. My faith was strengthened. I became more humble as I knew I was completely reliant upon the Lord. And I learned the value of fasting and praying often. I was being purified.

All of us go through trials, but we choose whether or not to let the adversity act as a purifying agent. Why not, if we have to pass through adversity anyway (which we all do) use these experiences to draw us closer to God? Why not see the growth opportunity in every circumstance that comes our way? Why not choose humility to help us overcome our weaknesses so we can joyfully navigate the hardship and come out of it purified and sanctified? Why not?

Precious metals, like gold, also go through a purification process. The process is much different for metals than it is for water, but it is equally taxing. For gold to become as pure as possible it takes intense heat as well as a dip into several chemicals. It's such an intense process that a person handling the purifying of the gold should completely cover up so as to not even breathe the fumes that come from the chemicals that are poured over the gold. The heat is so intense that specialized gloves are required to handle the tongs that handle the container that the gold is in. That is intense!

Just as the purification process is different for precious metals than it is for water, the purifying of our hearts will be individualized. But whatever process we must go through, we know it is necessary. Hearts become pure because instead of hardening them and becoming angry when difficulties arise, we choose to be like the Jaredites by humbling ourselves and praising God. A more purified heart is one reward for enduring well. And a purified heart is a worthy goal. Remember: "Blessed are the pure in heart: for they shall see God."[11]

Sanctification is as important as purification. The Old Testament prophet, Joshua, in preparation to take his people to Jordan, told them, "Sanctify yourselves: for to morrow the Lord will do wonders among you."[12]   In this instance, the Lord required individual holiness *before* He would provide the miracle. And so I ask myself: *What miracle is the Lord ready to give me, but is contingent upon my sanctifying myself first?* The miracle that took place for Joshua's people was their crossing what was previously a swollen river, on dry ground to safety. What is there in my life that is seemingly impossible right now, which if I sanctify myself, can become a true reality through Divine intervention? While we were fighting to keep our son, whom the government was insisting on taking away, we were reminded by our attorney that "the government isn't God." Many times throughout that experience I had to remind myself that God is in charge and that he can work mighty miracles. He does work miracles. Am I worthy to be the recipient?

How do we know if we've become sanctified? The scriptures have the answer: "Now they, after being *sanctified* by the Holy Ghost, having their garments made white, being pure and spotless before God, *could not look upon sin save it were with abhorrence.*"[13] How do we view sinful behavior? Do we tolerate it? Do we sometimes embrace it because it suits our situation? Do we look upon sin with apathy? When we get to the point where we can only be abhorred by sin, we will know that we have become sanctified. Remember though, that judging the sin is not judging the sinner. The people of Helaman were not only sanctified (thus they abhorred sin) but they were also humble. They recognized their own nothingness and sought for the welfare of their brethren (even those who were persecuting them) as much as they sought for their own. In fact, they became sanctified in part because they did not compare themselves with others and think poorly of sinners. As they "wax[ed] stronger and stronger in their humility and firmer and firmer in the faith of Christ"[14] they looked outward to serve, not to pass unrighteous judgment.

Purification and sanctification of our hearts is a result of choosing to use the gift of the Atonement. It comes as we turn our hearts to God and accept the enabling and strengthening power He offers through His grace. But there is one more step.

[1] Dictionary.com, Purify

[2] Dictionary.com, Sanctify

[3] The New Testament, 2 Corinthians 12:10

[4] The Old Testament, Job 23:10-11

[5] The Book of Mormon, Alma 34:32

[6] Doctrine and Covenants 121:8

[7] LDS General Conference, April 1980, God Will Have a Tried People, Howard W. Hunter

[8] The Book of Mormon, Ether 6:7

[9] The Book of Mormon, Ether 6:9

[10] The Book of Mormon, Ether 6:8

[11] The New Testament, Matthew 5:8

[12] The Old Testament, Joshua 3:5

[13] The Book of Mormon, Alma 13:11-12

[14] The Book of Mormon, Helaman 3:35

WHICH SANCTIFICATION COMETH BECAUSE OF THEIR YIELDING THEIR HEARTS UNTO GOD

I love knowing that there is a plan for each of us in mortality. It's exciting for me as I watch the plan designed for me unfold. I'm a person who loves surprises, so the anticipation of "what's next" is exciting. "The Lord has placed currents of divine influence in your life that will lead you along the individual plan He would have you fulfill here on earth,"[1] taught Elder Richard G. Scott. Even though there is a plan for us, we still are blessed with agency to choose. Elder Scott continued: "I do not fully understand how it is done, but this divine current does not take away your moral agency. You can make the decisions you choose to make." This is because one of the great gifts our Father has given to all of his children is agency. He will not force us to feel, think, or act in any given way. It has always been and will always be our choice.

Possessing agency can sometimes be a tough thing. It means that we are responsible not only for our choices, but also for the consequences. I was a freshman in high school when the pressure of agency weighed heavily upon me. It was the first day of marching band practice. Our teacher, Mr. D. (his last name was too hard for many to pronounce) was a gruff man. At least, that's how he appeared to brand new ninth graders. He may have been short, but he had a booming voice and a serious demeanor. He used our last names when calling roll and I sometimes felt like I was in boot camp. That first day, as we stood at attention in our ranks, Mr. D. shouted out the rules: Be on time! No gum chewing! Silence in the ranks! No excused absences from performances! And then he elaborated on the last one: The only excuse for missing any performance is death. Even sickness is not acceptable. It wasn't too long into the season when Mr. D. announced an upcoming parade. It was scheduled for a Sunday. I had been raised to understand that Sundays were holy days – days to set aside as a time for worship and rest. I was sure my parents would not allow me to march in a parade on a Sunday. I wondered how Mr. D. would react to a phone call from my parents, excusing me from that performance. Would he yell at them too? When I got home from school that day, I told my mom the problem. Would she like to write a note for me to give to Mr. D. or would she and Dad rather call him? Mom said it would be best to wait for Dad to come home and we could all talk about it together. That night, the three of us had a conversation. It didn't go at all how I expected. No, Mom wouldn't be writing a note for me; no, Dad wouldn't be calling Mr. D. I was old enough, they told me, to make my own decision. Whatever choice I made, they would support. I thought it was completely unfair that they chose that moment to make me grow up. They had no idea how mean Mr. D. was. If I chose to follow my heart in honoring the Sabbath Day I would fail the class for the entire semester! But I knew that if my parents got involved they could prevent something so horrendous. They refused. They expressed great confidence in me and knew that whatever I decided would be the best choice for that given situation. I felt like their confidence was misplaced. I went to bed that night without a clue as to what I would do. The next day in band class I worked up a sweat just thinking about my decision. I couldn't focus on the music. Mr. D. became a giant of a man as I imagined approaching him about *anything*, but especially if I chose to challenge one of his rules. I let a couple of days go by, each night my parents asking if I'd made a decision. Finally, the third night when they asked, I knew what I would do. I told my parents that, regardless of the outcome, I couldn't feel good about marching on a Sunday. My choice was made, but I was severely lacking courage. Having prayed mightily that night, I eventually fell asleep. The next morning I could barely eat. Leaving the house with my parents' vote of confidence, I was resolved to do what had to be done. At the completion of band class Mr. D. dismissed the students and walked into his attached office. I slowly gathered my things and when I was the only student left in the room, I guardedly approached the office door. I stood there for just a minute, hoping he would see me and I wouldn't have to knock. Looking up from his desk and taking notice of me, Mr. D. boomed, "What is it, Call?" I'm certain that there has never been more sincere pleading for divine help than there was at that moment from my heart. "Mr. D., could I talk with you about the Sunday parade?" Thus begun the conversation. Mr. D. leaned back in his chair, hands behind his head as his face softened while I spoke. I told him that I believed with my whole heart that Sunday is the Lord's day – a day of worship. I believed I would be breaking a commandment of God if I marched. I told him that I understood his rules and that he would give me a failing grade for missing the performance, but I loved band so much that I was hoping I could still attend the class. (Yes, I was a band nerd.) When I finished talking, Mr. D. stood from his chair, leaned across his desk and said, "I'll change the rule in class tomorrow. You may miss the performance and you will still pass the class. That's all." The next day in band class Mr. D. announced that there had been a change in the rules. One could be excused from a performance only if dead or if religious beliefs conflicted with the event. From that day on, each year when Mr. D. welcomed new students with his shouting of the rules, a conflict of religious beliefs stood as an acceptable reason to miss a performance. A post script to this experience is that Mr. D. became a favorite teacher of mine as well as my younger siblings. Our entire family got to know him and in the end, he wasn't the tyrant I thought he was. I learned during my band experience that with agency comes responsibility. I learned that heavenly help is available while exercising our agency, and that if I seek to align my will with Heavenly Father's will, He offers me His strength and support to carry out the decisions I make.

Elder Neal A. Maxwell taught the truth that "the submission of one's will is really the only uniquely personal thing we have to place on God's altar. The many other things we 'give,' brothers and sisters, are actually the things He has already given or loaned to us. However, when you and I finally submit ourselves, by letting our individual wills be swallowed up in God's will, then we are really giving something to Him! It is the only possession which is truly ours to give!"[2] The people of Helaman who "yield[ed] their hearts unto God" were actually submitting their will. This verse of scripture we've been studying throughout the book teaches us the path to sanctification. All the steps previously outlined (fasting, prayer, growing in humility and faith) prepare us to be able to submit to His will while in the midst of suffering. It's not really a submission if there is no hardship.

Consider the first family in the Book of Mormon. Lehi's family, all of them together, experienced the same exodus from their home, the same hardship through wilderness, the same searching for food. In short, they all experienced the same adversity and hardship. Yet some murmured throughout, dug in their heels, and resisted the entire experience.[3] Others submitted even though it was hard.[4] Through the struggles, they continued to grow in faith and humility. And those who did "submit cheerfully and with patience to all the will of the Lord"[5] became sanctified.

It is through suffering, adversity and hardship that we may become sanctified by Him who suffered all. "For it became him, for whom are all things, and by whom are all things, in bringing many sons unto glory, to make the captain of their salvation perfect through *sufferings*. For both he that sanctifieth and they who are sanctified are all of one: for which cause he is not ashamed to call them brethren."[6] It is the Lord who sanctifies us when we have proven ourselves by submitting our will to Him through our suffering. As mentioned in an earlier chapter, we will all suffer. It is a natural part of mortality. It is *how* we suffer that will determine our eternal destinies.

This one verse describing the situation of the people of Helaman succinctly outlines the path to sanctification. And each step outlined is interconnected. We must be humble to have our faith grow; we must fast and pray to become humble; we must serve to have our hearts purified. "Yielding one's heart to God signals the last stage in our spiritual development. Only then are we beginning to be fully useful to God!"[7] It is part of the divine plan for *all of us* to lift and serve each other and together rise to exaltation.

Like everything else in mortality, we learn to yield our hearts to God bit by bit as we practice in each progressive stage of life. That's what experience, adversity, opposition and hardship is for! It exists so we can practice yielding our hearts to God. We practice as we keep eternal perspective and the purpose of life forefront in our minds. And the happy news is this: It is possible, and even preferable, to experience joy throughout the *entire* process. "Men are that they might have joy,"[8] was taught by the prophet Nephi. Remember that joy goes beyond happiness. It can only exist in righteousness. As we jump on our personal paths by following the divine currents that Elder Scott taught us about, we are then able to experience real joy. And we stay on our paths when we learn to yield our hearts to God. "It is only by yielding to God that we can begin to realize His will for us. And if we truly trust God, why not yield to His loving omniscience? After all, He knows us and our possibilities much better than do we."[9] As we practice submitting our will to His, the burden of creating our own path disappears. We experience a freedom previously unknown. "This subjection to God is really emancipation,"[10] stated Neal A. Maxwell.

When we're doing our best to live righteously, even with the mistakes we make, progress is being made. We get better with each experience that we conquer. Not long ago, I was at the point in my life, with enough prideful experience behind me, that I knew I would be happiest if I truly desired Heavenly Father's will over my own. So I began an adventure working on a project that I felt good about. I felt inspired and directed as I moved along. Right near the point of completion, what I expected to happen didn't occur. Everything came to an abrupt halt. I wondered how I could feel so good about this, just to have it end before coming to fruition! I remembered the lessons I'd learned earlier in my life – times when I stubbornly pushed my agenda, rejecting the thought that Heavenly Father's plan could possibly be better than mine. I didn't want to experience that again. And so I fasted and prayed. I asked for humility and I meant it. I asked for understanding. Although I didn't get all the answers I hoped for, I was blessed with peace and the assurance that Heavenly Father is actively in my life. I was blessed to know that I had followed His direction. He wasn't necessarily telling me that the actions I was taking in this project would result in my expectations – but nonetheless, He was guiding me in those actions. The disappointment lessened and I began to feel more confident in my standing with God. I had done as He directed, and I didn't get angry, resentful, or bitter when the results weren't what I expected. I was learning to yield my heart to Him.

Now, each time something doesn't go the way I hope or expect it to go, I remind myself that I am practicing. What appears to be a result that I don't want is actually an opportunity for me to yield, to submit. In reality, the result will be the same whether I murmur or praise. I will choose to praise. I will practice yielding my heart to God so that someday I, too, may be sanctified.

[1] LDS General Conference, October 1999, He Lives, Richard G. Scott

[2] LDS General Conference, October 1995, Swallowed Up in the Will of the Father, Neal A. Maxwell

[3] The Book of Mormon, 1 Nephi 2:12, 1 Nephi 16:20, 1 Nephi 3:31, 1 Nephi 2:11-12,

[4] The Book of Mormon, 1 Nephi 3:7, 1 Nephi 2:16, 1 Nephi 2:3

[5] The Book of Mormon, Mosiah 24:15

[6] The New Testament, Hebrews 2:10-11 (italics added)

[7] LDS General Conference, April 1985, Willing to Submit, Neal A. Maxwell

[8] The Book of Mormon, 2 Nephi 2:25

[9] LDS General Conference, April 1985, Willing to Submit, Neal A. Maxwell

[10] LDS General Conference, April 1985, Willing to Submit, Neal A. Maxwell

Other books by Denalee Call Chapman:
CONQUERED
YOLO: Lessons Learned From Eve & Esther

Heartfelt thanks to Jennilyn Call Eckersley
Your editing and technical savvy has kept me sane.

DenaleeChapman.com

www.ingramcontent.com/pod-product-compliance
Lightning Source LLC
Chambersburg PA
CBHW071834020426
42331CB00007B/1726